PLAYING CARD DIVINATION
for BEGINNERS

Playing Card Divination for Beginners

Fortune Telling with Ordinary Cards

Richard Webster

2002
Llewellyn Publications
St. Paul, Minnesota 55164-0383, U.S.A.

First Edition
First Printing, 2002

Book design and editing by Joanna Willis
Cover design by Gavin Dayton Duffy
Cover photograph © 2002 by Digital Stock

Library of Congress Cataloging-in-Publication Data
Webster, Richard, 1946–
   Playing card divination for beginners: fortune telling with ordinary cards / Richard Webster.
      p.   cm.
   Includes bibliographical references.
   ISBN 0-7387-0223-4
    1. Fortune-telling by cards. I. Title.

  BF1878 .W43 2002
  133.3'242—dc21

                             2002073077

Llewellyn Publications
A Division of Llewellyn Worldwide, Ltd.
P.O. Box 64383, Dept. 0-7387-0223-4
St. Paul, MN 55164-0383, U.S.A.
www.llewellyn.com

Printed in the United States of America

ALSO BY RICHARD WEBSTER

Astral Travel for Beginners

Aura Reading for Beginners

The Complete Book of Palmistry

Dowsing for Beginners

Feng Shui for Beginners

Is Your Pet Psychic?

Llewellyn Feng Shui series

Omens, Oghams & Oracles

Palm Reading for Beginners

Pendulum Magic for Beginners

Practical Guide to Past-Life Memories

Seven Secrets to Success

Soul Mates

Spirit Guides and Angel Guardians

Success Secrets

Write Your Own Magic

For my good friends
Alan and Michele Watson

CONTENTS

Preface / xiii

Introduction / 1
    A History of Playing Cards

1 Essential Requirements / 17
    Preparing for a Reading

2 The Meanings of the Cards / 29
    The Joker
    Spades
    Hearts
    Diamonds
    Clubs

3 Learning the Cards / 91
    The Suits
    The Number Cards

The Court Cards
Putting It Together

4   How to Interpret Groups of Cards / 101

Predominance of Colors and Suits
Predominance of High and Low Cards
Card Combinations
Other Significant Combinations
Cards Flanked by Two Cards of the Same Suit

5   How to Read Your Own Cards / 113

Choosing Your Significator Card
A Sample Spread
Judelle's Reading

6   How to Read the Cards for Others / 127

A Sample Reading
Another Reading

7   Love and Romance / 143

Lucky Three
Advice from the Kings
Advice from the Queens
Will the Person of My Dreams Arrive
    in the Next Twelve Months?
Six Paths to Happiness

8   Other Spreads / 155

Past-Present-Future
Date of Birth Reading
Birthday Reading
Gypsy Spread
The Mystic Cross
Yes or No
The Sandwich
One-Two-Three-Four-Five
Once a Week
The Pyramid of Egypt

Afterword / 173

Appendix
 Dream Interpretation
 Using Playing Cards / 175

Guided by the Cards
Meditation Method
Gypsy Method

Notes / 187

Suggested Reading / 191

PREFACE

It was an old, gloomy, detached garage close to the beach. All day, every day, people came to have their cards read by a young man who seldom had anything to say, except when he was reading cards.

I loved watching him give readings. His appearance and manner subtly changed once he had a deck of cards in his hands. He became more confident and outgoing. The pleasure he received from giving readings was apparent in every move he made. He spoke with expression and with a strong, sure voice, frequently nodding his head to emphasize the points he wished to make.

One day I saw him in the street and asked him if he would teach me how to read cards. Away from the safety of his garage, he could not look me in the eye and mumbled an answer.

"I can't teach you. The cards talk to me."

Several years later, I was fortunate enough to observe Gypsy women reading cards. Their readings were quite different. They were more structured, and every card had a distinct meaning. They used a pack of thirty-two cards, as they did not use the two through six of any suit. Although they were reasonably friendly, they were not prepared to discuss their "dukkerin" (fortune telling) with me.

These two experiences, twelve thousand miles and several years apart, started me on a quest to learn more about the gentle art of reading playing cards. This book is the result.

INTRODUCTION

Peple have always wanted to see a glimpse of the future. Primitive people lived in a state of constant anxiety, as so many things were out of their control. Earthquakes, droughts, floods, thunderstorms, and wild animals were just some of these forces.

It is not surprising that primitive peoples sought ways to find out in advance what was going to happen. If they knew that, they could store food to sustain them during a drought, just as the pharaoh did at the time of the seven-year famine. They could move to higher ground before a flood occurred, or move away from an area that was to be destroyed by fire.

Of course, even though life has changed enormously, we still live in uncertain times. The fast pace of the lives we all lead creates as much anxiety as anything our ancestors experienced. People want to know if their jobs are secure, if relationships will last, if they have enough money for retirement. At every stage of life, people have questions about the future.

Nothing could be more fascinating and intriguing than the unknown, especially the mystery that surrounds the future. During the last few thousand years, many different systems have been used to predict the future. The movements of the planets, extremes of weather, lines on the palms of hands, bumps on the head, crystal gazing, dreams, and omens of all sorts are just some of the ways that have been used by people in attempt to part the veil of the future and see beyond now.

The Bible mentions a variety of methods of divination, including dreams, signs, and prophecy. Joseph saw visions from his early childhood (Genesis 37:5–11). Saul visited the witch of Endor (I Samuel 28:7–25). The king of Babylon consulted the teraphim, which were images used for the giving and receiving of oracles (Ezekiel 21:21).

A HISTORY OF PLAYING CARDS

No one knows exactly how or when playing cards were invented. However, there are two legends that may, or may not, describe their origin. The first claims that playing cards were invented in the twelfth century in the harem of the Chinese imperial palace. The women living there led lives of incredible boredom waiting to be summoned to the emperor's bed, and the legend says that in 1120 C.E. one of them invented playing cards to help pass the time.

The second legend claims that playing cards were invented in India. Apparently, one of the maharajahs constantly pulled at his beard. This habit annoyed his wife so much that she invented a game to utilize his hands.

These legends are charming, and may even hold a kernel of truth. However, it seems more likely that playing cards originated in Korea and were descended from a Korean divinatory arrow. At least two experts on the history of playing cards, Sir William Wilkinson and Dr. Stewart Culin, made a study of the Korean connection and were convinced that this is where playing cards began.[1]

Wilkinson and Culin were certain of this origin because the original Korean cards were similar in shape to the slips of bamboo that were used as arrows in divination rites. A scroll in the shape of a heart on the backs of the cards was thought to represent an arrow feather. Finally, it is thought that the numbers on the cards were related to the cock feathers on the arrows.[2]

It is possible that playing cards reached the West through Persia, as the designs on their cards included young men and women, and kings and queens on thrones. However, no one knows for certain if modern-day playing cards came from Korea, China, India, or Persia. In fact, it is possible that they were invented by a European, perhaps after seeing an Asian deck of cards.[3]

No matter where they came from, playing cards quickly spread throughout Europe in the second half of the fourteenth century. No one knows if they arrived in Italy or Spain first. The Moors occupied large parts of Spain at that time, but Italy was busy trading with the East, making it the more likely candidate.

Certain segments of the European community opposed playing cards from the start. The first prohibition against playing cards was probably issued in Bern in 1367. However, this is not based on conclusive evidence; it is mentioned in a list of legal documents that dates back to the end of the fourteenth century.[4]

A German monk named Johannes von Rheinfelden also mentioned playing cards in a Latin manuscript found in the British Museum. It says, "The game of cards has come to us in this year, viz., the year of our Lord 1377."[5] Rheinfelden described six different packs of cards, containing from fifty-two to sixty cards, each with four suits. Although he did not describe the suits, they were probably the traditional cups, swords, money, and clubs.

A few years later, playing cards were being mentioned in places as widespread as Paris, Florence, and Barcelona, usually because of a prohibition against them. It did not take the Christian church long to pronounce playing cards the work of the devil.

It is unlikely that playing cards were seen in Europe before about 1370, as Francesco Petrarch (1304–1374), Giovanni Boccaccio (1313–1375) and Geoffrey Chaucer (1343–1400) did not mention them in their writings. From all accounts, these men were enthusiastic about games and gambling, and it is inconceivable that they would not have mentioned playing cards if they had known of them. Petrarch wrote a treatise on gaming, and did not mention playing cards. Boccaccio and Chaucer both referred to other forms of gambling in their works, but failed to mention playing cards as well.

In 1363, an ordinance of the Catholic Church prohibited clerics from participating in games of chance. However, it did not specifically mention playing cards. Neither did an edict of King Charles V of France, dated 1369, which forbade certain sports and pastimes by name.

Many people believe that it was the Gypsies who introduced playing cards to Europe. However, this is not the case as playing cards preceded the Gypsies' arrival in Europe by more than twenty years. (The first Romanies appeared in Europe in 1398.) Other people claim that Marco Polo brought them back from China. Although the Chinese did have playing cards, they were totally different from the cards that were introduced into Europe. Another story is that the crusaders brought them back from the Holy Land. Unfortunately, the Crusades were over some seventy years before playing cards were first mentioned in Europe.

The oldest Tarot cards in existence were made for Charles VI of France. This has led people to speculate that Jacquemin Gringonneur, the man who made three decks of Tarot cards for the king, invented playing cards. This is not true either, as playing cards were well established by the time he made these decks in 1392.

The story of Charles VI and Tarot cards is an interesting one. Apparently, Charles VI suffered from periods of depression. Odette, his beautiful mistress, played the harp, sang, and read to him. She also constantly searched for anything that might amuse the king. One day she heard about playing cards, which were new to the city. After seeing them, she asked Jacquemin Gringonneur to design a special pack in which the principal cards depicted important people in the royal court. The deck is alleged to have brought the king out of his depression (at least temporarily), and the picture cards became known as "court cards."

The legend does not finish here. Shortly after the king had been helped by the playing cards, a Saracen woman visited Odette and taught her how to interpret and read the cards. Although Odette was supposed to keep her new skill a secret, word quickly got out, and fortune telling with cards became hugely popular. Some people were unhappy with this, especially when the cards picked out their infidelities. Consequently, they told the king that the cards created huge gambling losses and succeeded in having them banned.

A famous knight named Etienne de Vignoles—better known as "La Hire"—was unhappy with this ban. The cards had successfully told him that a certain lady loved him, something he would not have discovered on his own, and he resolved to repeal the king's edict. He succeeded by asking Jacquemin Gringonneur to create a patriotic deck of cards showing mythological gods and goddesses, Biblical figures, and past and present heroes. The four kings were Julius Caesar (diamonds), Charlemagne (hearts), Alexander the Great (clubs), and King Charles VI (spades). The queens were Pallas (also known as Minerva), the goddess of arms (spades); Judith the great biblical heroine (hearts); Rachel (of the Bible) (diamonds); and Argine the fairy (clubs), who looked exactly like Odette. (*Argine* is an anagram of "regina.")

La Hire also included himself in this pack of cards. He became the jack of hearts. The other jacks were Hogier the Dane (spades), Hector of Troy (diamonds), and Lancelot (clubs).

La Hire even gave the suits a military theme. The clubs depicted the sword crossguards, the hearts the tips of the crossbows, the diamonds the heads of the arrows, and the spades were the tools that were so useful in a siege. The king was delighted with the new pack and repealed the edict. In no time, cards were available everywhere again.[6]

The oldest known decks of cards are Tarot decks, and the standard decks of playing cards that we use today derive from them. Within a few years of their introduction, entrepreneurs began mass-producing playing cards using stencils. By eliminating the major arcana and the knaves, the pack was reduced to a deck of fifty-two cards, making them less expensive to manufacture and purchase.

The spread of playing cards alarmed the church and they began burning them in huge bonfires. This did nothing to diminish the demand for cards, and mass production brought the cost down to a more affordable level. In fact, in 1454, a pack of cards was purchased for the dauphin of France for five sous tournois. This was one-thousandth of the price the duke of Milan had paid for a deck thirty-nine years earlier.

As playing cards spread across Europe, different regions made changes to them. For instance, in the Italian decks the kings are depicted sitting down. In Spain, the kings are standing up. The Germans changed the suits entirely, choosing to use bells, hearts, leaves, and acorns, instead of the Italian swords, cups, coins, and clubs.

Wood engraving enabled playing cards to be produced more quickly, and with greater quality, than before. Then the invention of copper engraving enabled artists to incorporate more and more detail into the cards.

The first known copper engraver, known as Master of the Playing Cards, was born in the early fifteenth century, and had a major influence on the quality of playing cards. He was working in Mainz, Germany, at the same time as Johann Gutenberg, and it would be amazing if the two men had not known each other. In fact, it is possible that the Master of the Playing Cards worked for Johann Gutenberg.[7] If so, this shadowy figure is connected with two of the most important events in the history of playing cards: the invention of copper engraving and printing.

It was the French who gave us the suits that we know today.[8] Legend attributes this to Etienne de Vignoles, the French knight we have already met, who died in 1442. If this is true, the suits we know today were created in the first half of the fifteenth century.

The heart and spade were copied from the German heart and leaf. However, the leaf was turned ninety degrees to make it an upright spade. The club is probably an adaptation of the German acorn. The diamond, however, was an original creation. This shape was popular in France between the twelfth and fifteenth centuries in ecclesiastical pavements, and was chosen deliberately to depict the major divisions of society in a single deck of cards.

Consequently, hearts represented the church; spades could be read as spearheads, and represented the aristocracy, because spears were the weapons of knights; diamonds represented the chancel of the church, which is where the wealthy were buried; and clover (clubs) represented the peasantry, as it was a food for pigs.

The French card manufacturers were highly innovative. They quickly discovered that they could make the four kings, queens, and jacks from one woodblock or copper engraving, and simply stencil in the four suits later. This enabled them to create packs of cards much more quickly than their rivals in other parts of Europe. Not surprisingly, it wasn't long before card manufacturers all over Europe began using generic kings, queens, and jacks too.

Until the middle of the nineteenth century, the jacks were called knaves. At this time, the card manufacturers began placing indices on two or four corners of each card to indicate its value. The familiar *K* for king and *Q* for queen began at this time. However, *Kn* for knave was potentially confusing, and the card's name was changed to jack. Nowadays, of course, a knave is considered a rogue.

The joker is a nineteenth-century American addition, and can be related to the Fool card in Tarot. Euchre used to be an extremely popular card game in the United States (and still has a strong following today). In this game, the jack of the trump suit and the other jack of the same color are called the "Bowers." When euchre was first invented, another card was introduced, called the "Best Bower." Ultimately, it became known as the joker.[9]

The Gypsies were probably the first to use playing cards for divination purposes, and greatly aided the spread of playing cards throughout Europe. One of the first books on fortune telling with playing cards appeared in Germany in the 1480s. It is called *Eim Loszbuch Ausz der Karten*. The instructions tell the reader to shuffle the cards and remove one. He or she then looks up the meaning of the card in a book of fate.

In 1540, Marcolino da Forli published a book on card reading in Venice. This was the first book to explain the different layouts and interpretations that can be made with playing cards. His system, which appears to be entirely his own, used only the number cards.[10] Marcolino da Forli's system split the cards into various groups such as goodness, beauty, intelligence, death, wedlock, sloth, and humility. His system was able to answer almost any question. The questions answered in his book include: "Is the lady valued by him she adores?" and "Will he do better to take a beautiful or an ugly wife?"[11]

The origin of one of the earliest decks of playing cards devised for fortune-telling purposes is not known. John Lenthall, a famous English producer of novelty cards, reprinted it in 1712. It seems likely that the original version appeared in the late 1600s. Lenthall was good at promoting his products, and advertised these as "Fortune-telling Cards, pleasantly unfolding the good and bad luck attending human life. With Directions of the Use of the Cards."

The method for interpreting these cards is unusual and complicated. A list of questions is printed on one of the kings. Each question also contains a number.

The enquirer uses this number to receive an answer on one of the odd-numbered cards. He or she is then referred to an even-numbered card for a quotation allegedly from a famous sibyl of antiquity. As well as this, each card contains a great deal of symbolism. For instance, Merlin appears on the ace of clubs, and Hermes Trismegistus on the ace of spades. Dr. Faustus appears on the three of clubs. The king of hearts depicts Herod. Nimrod is on the king of diamonds. Pharaoh is on the king of clubs, and Holophernes is on the king of spades. The choice of famous people, both real and imaginary, is strange. Even Wat Tyler and Cupid are represented.

The John Lenthall fortune-telling cards were extremely popular from the first half of Charles II's reign until after the death of Queen Anne. Numerous editions of them, official and pirated, were made. Despite the success of John Lenthall's pack, however, cards made purely for fortune telling did not become popular in the rest of Europe until the end of the eighteenth century.

Arguably, the catalyst for this interest began with the publication of *Monde Primitif* by Antoine Court de Gébelin (1725–1784) in 1781. He claimed that Tarot cards were directly descended from the *Book of Thoth*, the mythical book that was believed to have been written by the Egyptian deity. A wave of books followed, which increased the interest in fortune telling with both Tarot and playing cards.

Court de Gébelin's book inspired thousands of people, including a wig-maker and fortune-teller named Alliette. He wrote *Manière de se récréer avec le jeu de cartes nomées Tarots* in 1783, and then produced his own deck of Tarot cards, known as the Etteilla deck. "Etteilla," his pseudonym, is a reversal of his own name. The Grand Etteilla Egyptian Gypsies Tarot deck is still available today.

Etteilla, in turn, inspired others. Throughout the nineteenth century many fortune-telling decks were produced. Probably the most famous of these was the Mlle. Lenormand deck, which is also still available.

Marie-Anne Lenormand (1768–1842) achieved both fame and fortune because of her skills at reading cards. She was considered the best fortune-teller in Paris when a young mother of two named Rose came to her for a reading. Rose had disguised herself as a maid, and watched with interest as Mlle. Lenormand cut and dealt the cards. In the European tradition, Mlle. Lenormand used a pack containing thirty-two cards. Rose listened silently as the fortune-teller told her that although there was sorrow ahead, there was also greatness. She was told that she would soon meet her second husband who would become the most powerful person in Europe.

Shortly afterward, a young general named Napoleon Bonaparte came for a reading. Mlle. Lenormand told him that he would marry a beautiful woman with two children. She also said that he would go to war in Italy, and return so triumphant that everyone in the country would know his name.

Napoleon did meet Rose, and fell in love. He did not like her name, though, and persuaded her to change it to Josephine. Shortly after that, they married. Josephine introduced the palm reader to the French court, and Mlle. Lenormand's practice thrived.

Joachim Murat, the king of Naples, came to Mlle. Lenormand for a reading. He was also the leader of Napoleon's cavalry. Mlle. Lenormand asked him to cut the cards. Murat turned over the king of diamonds. This card traditionally means treachery and deceit. Mlle. Lenormand replaced the card, shuffled the deck, and asked Murat to cut the cards again. He cut to the king of diamonds. The same thing happened on his third attempt. Mlle. Lenormand was furious and threw the cards at him, telling him that he would die on the gallows or in front of a firing squad. Her prediction was correct, and Murat was executed by firing squad in 1815.

Some years after his first consultation, Napoleon consulted Mlle. Lenormand again. Mlle. Lenormand told him that he was considering divorcing Josephine. She also told him to be careful of pride, as it could sweep him to the heights, but also bring him back down again.

Napoleon found Mlle. Lenormand too accurate. She was arrested on December 12, 1809, and imprisoned for twelve days. She was released only after the divorce had been finalized.

These events all helped to promote Mlle. Lenormand's practice. In 1818 she wrote a best-selling book titled *Mémoirs historique et secrets de l'Imperatrice Joséphine (Historical and Secret Memoirs of the Empress Josephine)*.

Mlle. Lenormand's deck contains a central picture, with three smaller pictures at the bottom of the card. The middle one of these is a plant or flower. The other pictures show domestic scenes, such as a man writing a letter, or a tutor teaching two children. In the top left-hand corner of the card is a playing-card index. Next to this is a planetary arrangement, and on the right-hand side is a letter and a planetary sign. This deck is commonly confused with a more modern German deck, known as the Lenormand fortune-telling deck. This deck of thirty-six cards contains pictures of different interpretations, with playing-card indices in a square or oval at the top of the cards.

The Book of Fate is an attractive French deck that dates from about 1890. It is still available today, but is now called *The Book of Destiny*. It contains thirty-two cards (each suit from eight to king, including aces), and an extra blank card to represent the querent. Each card has a picture that illustrates the meaning of the card. The nine of clubs, for instance, represents a gift or surprise. The king of hearts depicts a man of law, and ten of hearts represents marriage. The meaning of each card is printed in French and English at the bottom. In the top left-hand corner is a miniature playing card.

Special fortune-telling decks are still being produced today. However, most card reading over the last six hundred years has been done with a regular deck of playing cards.

Not surprisingly, a large amount of superstition is connected with playing cards. For instance, it is considered a sign of grave danger ahead if you drop an entire deck of cards on the floor. It is considered dangerous to carry a deck of cards on your person if you work in a potentially dangerous career, such as mining or seafaring. It is considered bad luck to throw old packs of cards away. Instead, they should be burned. While the old pack is burning, a new pack should be taken from its box and waved three times in the smoke. Cards that are used for fortune telling should never be used for card games, and vice versa. It is considered good luck to blow on a deck of cards before using them. Conversely, it is a sign of bad luck if a single black card drops to the floor. A run of black cards, either in a game or in a fortune-telling spread, is considered to be an omen of major misfortune.

one

ESSENTIAL REQUIREMENTS

Most card readers base their interpretations on the traditional meanings of each card. However, even experts argue about the precise meanings of the cards. Interpretations have changed over time, and from place to place. Consequently, if you buy ten books on reading playing cards you will find variations in the meanings for each card.

You will notice the same thing if you watch ten different card readers. The young man who read cards in a garage did not appear to know the meanings of each individual card. He looked at groups of cards and created his readings from these. The Gypsy women, on the other hand, seemed to rely purely on their interpretations of each individual card, and ignored combinations of cards. Also, in the European fashion, the Gypsies use only thirty-two cards rather than the entire deck.

These methods are completely different, yet they both produce large numbers of happy clients. How is this possible?

When the cards are mixed and dealt they create a pattern of cards that may appear to be random, but in fact is not. This may sound strange at first. Our subconscious minds are linked into the universe and have an awareness of the past, present, and future. Normally, this information is not made available to our conscious minds, except when we receive sudden flashes of intuition or dream precognitive dreams. Fortunately, we can gain access to this information by creating a special arrangement of cards that is directed by our subconscious minds. As our subconscious minds already know what the future will be, they can create an arrangement of cards that appears to be random, but is, in actuality, a picture of the future. The microcosm (the apparently random arrangement of cards) reflects the macrocosm (the universe). Naturally, many other items can be used instead of cards. Dice, bones, and dominoes are three popular examples of objects that are used to create apparently random patterns that are then interpreted.

Of course, in this book we are concerned with fortune telling with playing cards. The basic concept is that, most of the time, the course of the future can be changed. The cards reveal the client's problems, and in the discussion that follows, the reader and the client can look at the difficulties in a different way. A sensitive reader will help clarify the problems, and allow the client to make his or her own decisions about the future.

The real skill of the reader is his or her ability to interpret the individual cards and the patterns they create in a manner that is helpful and useful for the client. As well as this, a good reader will have empathy toward his or her clients and will pick up on feelings and intuitions that can be used to enhance the reading.

Naturally, this is complicated by the fact that people want to hear good news about the future. People may say they want to hear everything—good and bad—but deep down they really only want to hear good news.

The cards act as a bridge between the reader and the client. They help build rapport. Consequently, they need to be handled and treated with respect. This applies even after the reading. Look after your cards. Keep them wrapped in a cloth, or in a box reserved purely for them. Replace them when they become old or dirty. Handle a new deck of cards for several minutes before using them for the first time to imprint them with your energies. Always treat your cards as if they were valuable and prized objects, and insist that your clients do the same. Refuse to read the cards for people who take it as a joke. You can have fun while giving the readings, but basically it is a serious process because the course of people's lives are involved.

No two card readers interpret the cards in exactly the same way. The cards provide pieces of a story, and it is up to the individual reader to interpret these and provide an accurate and satisfying reading. It is then up to the client to make any necessary changes to achieve the outcome that he or she desires.

In this book we will look at a number of different methods of card reading. Experiment with these, and decide which method you like the best. With practice and a caring, gentle manner toward your clients, you will ultimately be able to give honest, revealing, and useful readings.

In this book I have also tried to provide the underlying basic meaning of each card. These have changed over the years. At the end of the eighteenth century when Mlle. Lenormand was plying her trade, the suits had the following meanings:

Spades were a sign of unhappiness, sufferings,
     sorrow, and death.

Hearts indicated happiness, friendship, love, and family matters.

Diamonds indicated business matters, travel, and news.

Clubs indicated money matters.

Today, the main change is that diamonds are considered the money cards, and spades are not considered to be quite as evil as before. For comparison, here is how the cards are interpreted today:

Spades indicate obstacles.

Hearts indicate love, romance, good fortune, and happiness.

Diamonds indicate money and financial transactions.

Clubs indicate hard work, variety, and friendships.

Mlle. Lenormand would have agreed with only some of the conventional interpretations. Traditionally, the king of spades was considered to be a wicked man or a magistrate; the queen of spades was a widow or evil woman; and the jack of spades was a spy or someone pretending to be someone he is not. The king of hearts was an influential man; the queen of hearts was a fair woman; and the jack of hearts was a studious and industrious young man. The king of diamonds was a fair and honest countryman; the queen of diamonds was a countrywoman; and the jack of diamonds retells news brought by a stranger. Finally, the king of clubs was a dark and evil man; the queen of clubs was a dark woman with a vicious tongue; and the jack of clubs was a dark, spendthrift youth.

Mlle. Lenormand considered the king of clubs to be a generous and obliging man, the total opposite to what other card readers of the time were saying. She also considered the queen of clubs to be gentle, affectionate, and loving; the king of diamonds was wicked and dangerous, while his wife was amoral, and the jack of diamonds was a young person intent on mischief.

This shows how different people have always interpreted the cards in their own ways. You will find it best to study and learn one method, and then experiment with others. Over a period of time, you will probably develop a system that is uniquely your own. No matter what system you use, the knowledge you gain will enable you to give good, sensitive readings to your clients.

PREPARING FOR A READING

It is important that you are mentally prepared to give a reading. You might like to take a few deep breaths to let go of any stress or tension that has built up over the day. You must be prepared to focus exclusively on your client and his or her needs for the duration of the reading. Consequently, any problems you may have yourself need to be put aside and temporarily forgotten. Put the person you are reading for at ease, and indulge in some small talk before starting the reading.

Some readers tell their clients to make a wish before the reading starts. I do not like this idea, as usually the client will not have anything specific in mind and will think of something frivolous or unimportant.

Handle the cards while talking to the client. This helps rid the cards of any memories of previous readings, and imbues them with your energies.

Before starting the reading, you need to choose the card that best symbolizes your client. The following are traditional interpretations for all of the court cards:

The suit of **spades** symbolizes people with dark hair and dark eyes.

The suit of **clubs** symbolizes people with brown hair and brown eyes.

The suit of **hearts** symbolizes people with light-brown hair and gray or blue eyes.

The suit of **diamonds** symbolizes people with blonde or red hair.

For a woman you would choose the queen of the appropriate suit, and for a man, the king. The jack is used to represent a young person of either sex. This means that a teenager would be represented by a jack. However, someone as old as thirty could still be represented by a jack, depending on his or her maturity and approach to life. Some people seem to be born middle-aged, while other people remain youthful until the day they die. You can use the time spent in preliminary conversation to decide whether or not to use a jack to represent your client.

Place the card that represents the client in the center of the area on which you will be doing the reading. This card is called the significator card, as it signifies the client.

Continue to mix the cards. When you feel ready, pass the cards to your client and ask him or her to shuffle them. It is important that the cards be mixed slowly in an overhand shuffle. The cards should not be riffle shuffled together. This is an effective way of shuffling the cards when playing card games, but is not appropriate in a reading situation. I often mime the actions of an overhand shuffle to ensure that the client handles the cards properly.

Allow the client to shuffle the cards for as long as he or she wants. Take them back, and hold them for a few moments before starting to deal out the spread. Some readers close their eyes and say a small prayer at this stage. You might like to ask for divine protection for you and the client, and ask that nothing but good ensues as a result of the reading.

Every now and again, someone will drop a card or two while shuffling the pack. As nothing happens by accident, these cards will have dropped for a reason. Consequently, they need to be studied and interpreted. I usually do this as soon as they have been dropped. However, at other times I have placed them to one side and read them along with the other cards in the spread.

There are many ways to lay out or spread the cards. The simplest method is to randomly select a single card and interpret that. The other extreme is to lay out every card in the deck. Most card spreads use some, but not all, of the cards.

A good, general-purpose spread that I use regularly consists of fifteen cards (Figure 1). It provides a comprehensive reading, and is an ideal spread to start with. The cards are dealt faceup from the face-down deck. The first two cards are placed on either side of the significator card. While I am dealing these cards I tell the client that these three cards represent him or her and the nature of the problems he or she is facing. In other words, they represent the present situation.

The next three cards are placed in a diagonal row heading upward and to the left from the first three cards. This creates the first of four spokes to an imaginary wheel surrounding the first three cards. Again, the

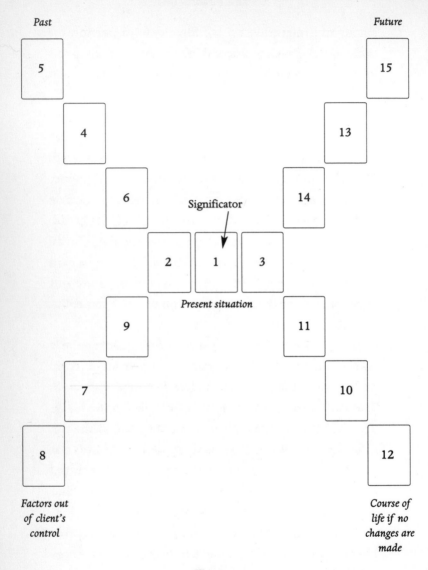

Figure 1
All-purpose spread.

first card is placed in the middle, with the other two cards placed on either side of it. While dealing these I tell the client that these cards reveal something of his or her past.

The next group of three cards is dealt in a diagonal row heading downward and to the left from the first three cards dealt. I tell the client that these cards represent factors that are out of his or her control.

The next three cards are dealt in a diagonal row heading diagonally downward and to the right. I tell the client that these cards indicate what will happen if he or she makes no changes in his or her life.

The final three cards are dealt diagonally upward and to the right from the first three cards dealt. While dealing these I tell the client that they indicate the future.

Some readers prefer not to deal all the cards out together after they have been mixed. While they take the top card and place it to the left of the significator card, the client shuffles again. Once this shuffle is finished, the reader takes a second card and places it in position and the client shuffles again. This process is continued until all of the cards are dealt. You might prefer to deal the cards this way. I used this method for a long time, but came to the conclusion that it was better to spend the extra time gained by dealing the cards out myself on the client's problems.

There is no hurry to start reading. Pause and look over the spread before starting to interpret the cards. I should mention at this stage a pet hate of mine. Many readers look at the spread of cards and make comments such as, "What a shame you don't have a three of diamonds," or, "If only we could exchange that card with the queen of clubs." There is no point in making comments of this sort. You have to deal with the cards that have been dealt. Any other cards are irrelevant to this particular reading.

In the next three chapters you will learn the meanings of the individual cards, and the more important groupings that can be made with them. Once you have mastered that, we will start reading and interpreting the cards.

two

THE MEANINGS OF THE CARDS

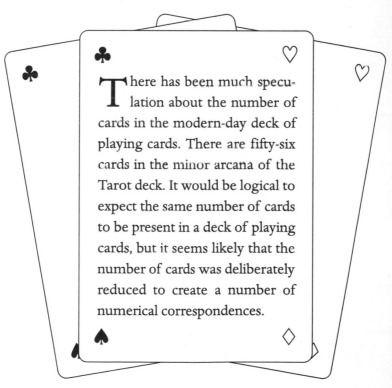

There has been much speculation about the number of cards in the modern-day deck of playing cards. There are fifty-six cards in the minor arcana of the Tarot deck. It would be logical to expect the same number of cards to be present in a deck of playing cards, but it seems likely that the number of cards was deliberately reduced to create a number of numerical correspondences.

For instance, in a twenty-four hour period, we have both night and day. A deck of playing cards contains red and black cards to depict this. There are four seasons in a year, which relates to the four suits. Naturally, spring and summer relate to the red cards, while the black cards represent fall and winter. There are also thirteen cycles of the moon in the course of a year. Each suit contains thirteen cards. There are 365 days in a year. If you add up the numerical value of each card (four ones, four twos, etc.) the total is 364. By adding the joker to this, you have a total of 365.

Life itself has been related to the four suits. Childhood can be symbolized by the hearts, youth by the diamonds, middle age by the clubs, and old age by the spades.

A little-known fact about playing cards is that the number of letters that make up a suit when each card is spelled out add up to fifty-two (ace, two, three, four, five, six, seven, eight, nine, ten, jack, queen, king). The exact same total is reached when the numbers of letters are added up in Dutch, French, and German as well.

There is a famous story concerning a soldier and his deck of cards that is believed to date back to the seventeenth century.[1] Richard Middleton was found looking at a deck of cards in church, and was taken to the mayor to explain his actions. He said to the mayor that the "pack of cards is both Bible, Almanack and Prayer Book to me."[2] He proved it by demonstrating how each card was somehow connected with the Bible. In the 1950s, Wink Martindale, Tex Morton, and several other country music singers recorded this story as a song called "Deck of Cards."

Each card has a specific meaning, but the interpretation of it can vary depending on the cards that are surrounding it in the spread. Also, as you become more familiar with the cards, you will find that certain cards develop special meanings for you. It is important to follow these hunches or feelings, as this information will be coming to you from your subconscious mind.

The four suits—spades, hearts, clubs, and diamonds—all relate to the four classes of people in the world at the time the cards were invented. At the top were the aristocracy (dukes, princes, earls, barons, etc.), followed by church leaders (bishops, abbots, priors, etc.). In third position were the merchants and administrators, followed by the largest group, the farmers and peasants. Their associations to the suits are as follows:

Aristocracy = Spades

Church = Hearts

Administrators and merchants = Diamonds

Farmers and peasants = Clubs

These divisions create keywords that can help us to understand the basic meanings of the cards. The spades, for instance, are dominating cards. The aristocracy was powerful, greedy, and ambitious. They made the laws and also enforced them. They were expert politicians, and success and failure for them related to how well they could determine future trends.

The cards in the suit of hearts relate to the Christian ideals of love, peace, cooperation, humility, and fairness.

The cards in the diamonds suit relate to the business side of life. This is where the administrators and merchants excelled. They knew how to buy something at a good price and sell it at a profit. Consequently, the cards in this suit relate to business dealings, financial undertakings, and success in commerce.

The cards in the suit of clubs relate to the peasants— that vast army of overworked, underappreciated, uneducated people who worked with their hands. These people suffered most under the feudal system. They enjoyed singing, dancing, playing games, gambling, drinking, and being at one with the soil. The cards in the clubs suit relate to persistence, growth, simple pleasures, and a belief that life will get better.

Cartomancers (the term given to people who tell fortunes with playing cards) have always been aware that the people they read for are complex beings who contain some of the qualities of each suit. This is demonstrated clearly in the Magician card in the Tarot deck. Many decks show the Magician standing behind a table holding a wand. On the table are a sword, cup, and a coin. These represent the four suits of the Tarot deck and show that a complete person contains all four suits in his or her makeup.

THE JOKER

 Some readers discard the joker, and I have had many lengthy discussions concerning the pros and cons of using it in readings. Certainly, the joker can complicate an otherwise straightforward reading, but as it appears only when necessary, I feel the joker should be left in the deck.

The joker depicts someone who follows his or her own path. This person is independent, unconventional, in touch with nature, and free of fear. Very often, this person is on a spiritual path that is at odds with the people surrounding the client. This card is nonmaterialistic. In fact, it is a warning for the client to take extreme care with financial matters.

Many years ago, I read the cards several times for an acquaintance of mine who was contemplating a major change in his way of life. He wouldn't tell me what he intended to do, but the joker appeared in every reading. Consequently, I knew he was planning something completely different to the conventional life he had always led. I was not surprised when he left home and joined a volunteer humanitarian aid program in Africa.

When the joker is found in the first three cards of the spread, it shows that the client has come to terms with him- or herself. This person is free of petty jealousies and small-mindedness, and is free to progress in the way best suited for him or her.

SPADES

Section of medieval society: Aristocracy
Planet: Mars
Element: Fire
Tarot card equivalent: Swords

Traditionally, the spades have represented difficulties, misfortunes, illnesses, and negativity. All the cards in the spades suit are related to change in one form or another. Consequently, the keyword for this suit is "change."

Ace of Spades

This is potentially the most powerful card in the deck. Unfortunately, it has received a bad name over the years because it is considered to be a prediction of death or disaster. It is easy to see how this superstition began, as the ace of spades represents tremendous force, energy, and power. When used positively, this energy can help the client accomplish great things, but when used negatively, it can just as easily destroy and harm. This card means that changes are in store, and the client needs to think carefully before acting. If he or she acts with a pure heart, the outcome will be a happy one.

If this card is one of the first three cards in the spread, it is a sign that the client possesses great power and should use it wisely. The client will have leadership skills and the potential to sway and influence others. However, the client may also be rigid, stubborn, and hard to get along with.

King of Spades

The king of spades represents a strong and powerful man. He is intelligent, honest, loyal, ambitious, and practical. His outlook is mature. If the client is male, this card may represent him, especially if it is found amongst the first three cards of the spread. If the client is female, this card represents a strong male influence in her life. This could be a father, brother, husband, relative, or close friend. If this card is one of the first three cards dealt, it indicates that this male presence has been around the female client for a long time.

The man represented by this card tries to be a good person, but tends to see everything in terms of right and wrong. He finds it hard to see other people's points of view as he is so convinced that his way is the best. He relies on logic and tends to ignore his intuition. He craves female company, but finds it hard to express his deepest feelings.

Queen of Spades

The queen of spades represents a woman of hidden depths. She is mysterious, intriguing, and enigmatic. Because she is reserved, it takes time to get to know her. However, it is well worth making the effort. She values her friendships, and enjoys helping the special people in her life. She is naturally intuitive and is quick to detect dishonesty and deceit. She is supportive, wise, and generous with the people she cares about. She has the potential to inspire others and encourage them to achieve things they would never have thought possible. The queen of spades makes a good friend, but she can also be a formidable enemy to people who have tried to deceive her.

If the client is a woman, this card can represent her if it is one of the first three cards dealt. If the client is male, this card usually represents his mother if it is one of the first three cards dealt.

The queen of spades seldom symbolizes love and romance. She is more likely to be a mentor or someone the client would go to for advice.

Jack of Spades

The jack of any suit indicates a young person of either sex. He or she is lighthearted, friendly, and curious. However, this person is likely to also be a dabbler, and his or her enthusiasms do not last for long.

The client is likely to know who this person is. If not, the reader will have to use his or her intuition to determine the sex of this person. The jack of spades frequently indicates a love interest. This person will be important to the client, but he or she may have doubts about the long-term future of the relationship, as the jack is more interested in the here and now, rather than thinking further ahead.

If the client is female, the jack will be male.[3] This young man will be ambitious, good with his hands, and be prepared to work hard once he settles down. The client will have to help him mature.

If the client is male, the person represented by the jack will be female. She will be possessive, surprising, intuitive, and contradictory. Consequently, the relationship will be exciting, but is unlikely to be smooth. The client may sometimes feel as if he or she is on a roller coaster ride.

Ten of Spades

The ten of spades represents a blockage or a dead end. It is traditionally considered the card of disappointment. It means that something the client has been working on can progress no longer, unless he or she is prepared to make a change of direction. Many people are reluctant to do this, and will blame themselves or others for their misfortune. The lesson of this card is to step back, pause, re-evaluate, and decide where to go from here. Once this has been done, the client can make a new start and ultimately achieve success.

Nine of Spades

Traditionally, the nine of spades is known as the card of disappointments. It is related to the Tower card in the Tarot deck. Consequently, it is frequently considered to be a card of total destruction, but this is only partially true.

The nine of spades indicates a change caused by unexpected means. This could be a physical change, but it could also indicate a change in the way in which the client thinks and looks at life. Most people fear change and will do almost anything to avoid it. The changes brought by the nine of spades are inevitable, and usually have a profound effect upon the future life of the client. They will make him or her more considerate and caring toward others, and they are also likely to make room for new opportunities.

Eight of Spades

The eight of spades is a joyful card, indicating contentment, happiness, and rest. The client will deserve this as he or she has worked hard to achieve a degree of material success. It is a fortunate sign to see this card anywhere in the spread. The client needs to be advised to make the most of this card, but not to spend too long enjoying the pleasures it provides. This is because some people are inclined to wallow in the pleasures and forget about their responsibilities.

Seven of Spades

The seven of spades indicates partial success. This can be frustrating, as often the client will have worked hard for a long time, and will consequently expect more in the way of rewards than he or she ultimately receives. The client will have to step back, reassess the situation, and then move forward again in a slightly different direction. The client will need time to reflect, think, and learn from this experience. This card promises long-term success, but only after a lengthy period of sustained effort.

Six of Spades

The six of spades indicates a time of patient waiting. This can be difficult, as the client will want to progress with his or her goals, but is, instead, marking time. This card can indicate ill health, either for the client or someone close to him or her.

The best way for the client to handle this situation until the necessary changes occur is to become involved with other interests, especially home and family matters, until this time of waiting is over.

Five of Spades

Traditionally, the five of spades is considered to be the card of tears. It can mean a time of grief, regrets, remorse, and separation. However, most of the time the client will have deliberately made the changes that caused these feelings to occur because he or she felt hemmed in or restricted. The reader needs to look at the cards surrounding the five of spades to see if these changes ultimately bring happiness or sadness.

Four of Spades

The four of spades represents peace, quiet, contemplation, and healing. It is, in effect, a rest after a period of difficulty or hard work. It allows the client time to regain energy and to work out where to go from here. This pause will be brief, but valuable.

Three of Spades

The three of spades is a card that depicts quick, sudden action, usually involving a communication of some sort. The problem with this is that the action is likely to be taken without sufficient forethought. The client should be advised to think before acting. Sometimes the action is done to the client. In this case, the client should deliberately step back and allow a period of time to pass before acting or reacting. This enables him or her to handle the situation calmly. If the client reacts immediately, he or she is likely to make the situation worse.

Two of Spades

The two of spades indicates a temporary hiccup. The client needs to be advised not to overreact, as the inconvenience is only temporary and is not of great importance. A gentle, tactful response will smooth troubled waters, and is likely to also enhance the client's reputation.

HEARTS

Section of medieval society: Clergy
Planet: Venus
Element: Water
Tarot card equivalent: Cups

Not surprisingly, all the cards in the hearts suit relate to emotions, feelings, love, romance, and friendship. When a large number of hearts appear in a spread, it is an indication that your client needs relationships with others in order to be happy. Consequently, the keyword is "love."

Ace of Hearts

Traditionally, the ace of hearts is known as the "home card." It is a card that promises joy, happiness, and pleasure. This happiness should always be shared with family and friends. All the aces are powerful cards, with a great deal of force and energy behind them. Consequently, the joy could be a strong, passionate, romantic relationship. It could mean a love affair with a new hobby or interest. It could even indicate a spiritual awakening. No matter what this card produces, great happiness will follow.

Traditionally, this card is related to young love, and is a sign of marriage and children. However, the meaning of this card is much broader than that, and has as much relevance in a spread done for an eighty-year-old as it is does for one prepared for a teenager.

King of Hearts

The king of hearts symbolizes a strong man who is wise, good-natured, reliable, fair, and open-minded. He may conceal his feelings beneath a gruff exterior. This is because he finds it hard to express his innermost thoughts and feelings. He is usually considered to be an older man because he is mature in outlook and approach. However, his physical age is unimportant.

This card could indicate the client, if he is an older man. This is especially the case when this card is found amongst the first three cards dealt. Frequently, this card indicates the client's father, or a strong authority figure. If the king of hearts is one of the first three cards dealt for a female client, it is a sign that her life will be closely connected with this man, who may be her father, husband, mentor, confidante, or even son.

Queen of Hearts

The queen of hearts is a lighthearted, carefree, and emotional woman. She is naturally intuitive, and is constantly full of exciting and different ideas. She uses her intuition to understand, motivate, and support the people she cares about. She appreciates beauty, and dislikes anything that is ugly, coarse, or inharmonious. She is sensitive and easily hurt. However, she does not carry grudges and is quick to forgive.

The queen of hearts enjoys good company and is friendly, gregarious, and sociable. She is quick to laugh and enjoys small talk.

If this card is one of the first three cards dealt to a female client, it is a sign that she already possesses many of the qualities of the queen of hearts. It is equally as fortunate for this card to be one of the first three dealt for a male client. It is a sign that he is loved. In this instance, the queen of hearts could symbolize his entire family.

Jack of Hearts

This card is traditionally considered to represent love and romance. However, it can also indicate a pleasant break in the normal day-to-day routine. This can range from a wonderful vacation to an enjoyable night out.

However, the jack of hearts is inclined to overindulge. Consequently, if he is one of the first three cards dealt in a spread, it is a sign to set goals, look ahead, and focus on the future rather than on immediate pleasures.

Ten of Hearts

The ten of hearts is a sign that good news is on its way. This news will usually be a direct response from something the client has initiated, but is sometimes totally unexpected. The nature of the news can usually be determined from the cards on either side of this one in the spread. The client needs to be advised that the good news is likely to be temporary, and he or she should enjoy it but not expect it to continue indefinitely.

Nine of Hearts

The nine of hearts is the happiest card in the entire deck. Traditionally, it is known as the "wish card." It shows that the client is growing and developing in all areas of his or her life, and that this joy and happiness is richly deserved. The client is likely to be deriving pleasure and satisfaction from helping others in some way. This card also indicates significant spiritual growth. The only thing that can mar the presence of this card is if the client overemphasizes the materialistic side of his or her life.

Eight of Hearts

The eight of hearts symbolizes a gift or offering. The client will either receive or give this gift. In either case, it will be received with pleasure. This gift will usually be a material object. However, it is just as likely to be a gift of time, love, friendship, wisdom, or peace of mind. If this card is one of the first three cards dealt in the spread, it is a sign that gifts will be both given and received.

Seven of Hearts

This card is traditionally considered a card of disagreement, usually a lover's quarrel. It frequently signifies a temporary altercation between two people who love each other. The period they spend apart will be valuable, as they will both have time to think about and learn from the experience. If this card is one of the first three dealt, it is a sign that the client is overly trusting or naïve, and needs to become more assertive and confident.

Six of Hearts

The six of hearts is a card that promises slow, steady improvement. Usually, this relates to relationships with people the client loves. The slowness of the improvement is likely to be frustrating, as most people seek instant gratification. This card can also be interpreted as a warning against impatience or taking shortcuts toward one's goal.

Five of Hearts

The five of hearts signifies a major change in a relationship. It usually means that something comes to an end. As this card relates largely to love, this might signify the end of a love affair. However, it could also indicate a business failure, or letting go of a once-important goal. This card indicates a temporary setback. The client will mourn the loss for a while, but will then bounce back and carry on with his or her life with new zest and enthusiasm.

Four of Hearts

The four of hearts is a rewarding card. It signifies that the client will receive satisfaction and pleasure from helping others, especially people he or she loves. The client is also likely to be happy in his or her work. The client will be busy in all areas of his or her life, and will have a sense of purpose.

Three of Hearts

The three of hearts relates to setbacks and disappointments, usually in love. It means that the client needs to be aware of difficulties ahead and take a more serious view of the current situation. Often the difficulties will be caused because the client spoke out of turn. Consequently, the client needs to think carefully before acting.

Two of Hearts

The two of hearts indicates the quiet pleasures that the client can experience in his or her life, usually time spent with the one person most important to the client. Often, these happy moments are overlooked, and this card shows that the client needs to learn to appreciate them more than he or she does at present. Traditionally, this card is related to good news concerning love and romance.

DIAMONDS

Section of medieval society: Administrators and merchants
Planet: Jupiter
Element: Air
Tarot card equivalent: Pentacles

The diamonds relate to business, power, and finance. Perseverance, logic, and hard work are also characteristics of this suit. Consequently, the keyword for this suit is "money."

Ace of Diamonds

Traditionally, this card has been related to the start of money coming in. This is extremely positive, as once the money starts, it has the potential to keep on coming. However, the meaning is much broader than this. Rather than money, the client might be gaining knowledge, wisdom, or spiritual insight. He or she might be discovering hidden talents that will ultimately produce money, status, or recognition. The client will be aware of increased energy and enthusiasm that will help him or her reach new levels of success.

If the ace of diamonds is one of the first three cards in a spread, it is a sign that the client is about to be given an opportunity to use his or her ability in a practical way that will bring credit and advancement.

King of Diamonds

The king of diamonds depicts an intelligent, shrewd, quick-witted, and complex man. He is impatient and constantly seeks new challenges. He is good at business, but prefers the overall view to the details. He is loyal to his family and friends, but can be harsh on people he does not trust or respect. He gives an impression of confidence and self-assurance, but deep down has doubts about himself. Consequently, he is easily hurt.

If this card is one of the first three cards dealt in a spread for a male client, it is a sign that he possesses many of the attributes of the king of diamonds. He should be advised to use tact and patience in his business activities, and to think carefully before speaking.

If this card is one of the first three cards dealt in a woman client's spread, it is a sign that she has met, or shortly will meet, a man with many of these characteristics. It would pay her to look more closely at the men in her life to ensure that she has not overlooked someone with the potential to bring her enormous happiness and personal satisfaction.

Mlle. Lenormand did not like this card and related it to treachery and deceit.

Queen of Diamonds

The queen of diamonds is passionate, demonstrative, and full of energy. She has an agile mind that can sum everything up at a glance. She is quick to act and has the potential to do well in business, or any other field that attracts her interest. She is a good friend who constantly motivates and inspires others. She is aggressive and loud when she feels she is being hemmed in or restricted.

If this card is one of the first three cards dealt in a male client's spread, it is a sign that he will shortly meet, or has met, a strong woman who will become a valuable ally.

If this card appears as one of the first three in a woman client's spread, it is a sign that she contains many of the traits of the queen of diamonds in her own makeup. She needs to be more decisive, less easily hurt, and choose a worthwhile goal for herself.

Jack of Diamonds

The jack of diamonds symbolizes someone who is not sure where to go from here. The person can be male or female, and is not necessarily young. Outwardly, this person may be giving an impression that everything is going well with his or her life, but inwardly there is conflict, confusion, and uncertainty. This card is sometimes related to the Hanged Man in the Tarot deck, and the analogy is apt, as both cards symbolize someone who is looking back and is fearful of moving forward.

If this card is one of the first three dealt, it means that it represents the client, or someone close to him or her. Patience is required whenever this card appears. As much time as is necessary should be allowed to enable the jack to resolve his or her difficulties, and to determine future directions.

Ten of Diamonds

The ten of diamonds indicates that the client pays too much attention to the material side of life. The client is likely to feel bored and unsettled and will want to escape from his or her humdrum, everyday life. He or she will be seeking new opportunities to explore and develop.

If this card is one of the first three dealt, it is a sign that the client is becoming cynical and disillusioned with the material world, and is seeking to explore other areas of life.

Nine of Diamonds

The nine of diamonds is an intriguing card that means that the client's wishes will come true. However, it is not always considered a positive card. In Scotland, for instance, this card is called the "curse of Scotland" because in 1692 the earl of Stair used it to give coded instructions before the infamous Glencoe Massacre.[4]

Mlle. Lenormand also considered this to be a card of danger. She had many large paintings on the walls of her impressive waiting room. One of these showed her pointing at the nine of diamonds while staring at a young army officer. This was General Charles de la Bédoyère, who was executed in 1815.[5] Interestingly, the Gypsies also interpret this card as a sign of deceit and dishonesty.

Because of these negative connotations, it is important that the client wishes for something worthwhile and honorable. Frivolous or selfish wishes are likely to rebound on the client.

Eight of Diamonds

The eight of diamonds is a portent of financial success, along with a balanced approach to life. It is a practical card that shows that the client will keep his or her feet on the ground and will not allow success to change him or her. The client may need to allow time to rest and relax, as he or she is likely to overwork.

Seven of Diamonds

The seven of diamonds indicates delays, setbacks, and confusion. Usually these problems relate to money, although they could appear in any area of the client's life. Most of the time, the problem is not as important as the client thinks. If he or she could step back from the problem and look at it from another point of view, a solution would be found. However, as long as the problem remains, the client's life is effectively put on hold. This will be a learning experience for the client. Most of the time, the cards on either side of the seven of diamonds will reveal which area of life the problem involves.

Six of Diamonds

The six of diamonds is a happy card indicating a warm, loving home and family life, with reasonable financial security. The client will be able to improve the family's financial situation if he or she is prepared to leave the close family environment and seek opportunities elsewhere. However, the cost in terms of home and family life will be high.

Five of Diamonds

The five of diamonds indicates a difference of opinion regarding financial matters. If the client is in a partnership situation, the two people might have differing views on how to deal with their money. This card can also indicate a sudden change in the client's fortunes.

Four of Diamonds

The four of diamonds is a sign of slow, steady progress toward a financial goal. It is achieved through thrift, hard work, and good money management. As the client's fortunes improve, so will his or her status and reputation.

Three of Diamonds

The three of diamonds relates to communications concerned with money. These are likely to be legal papers, a contract, or perhaps a will. The outcome of this communication will be determined by the card that is to the right of the three of diamonds in the spread. If there is no card in this position, it is a sign of confusion. The outcome will be delayed and will not bring as much satisfaction as the querent would wish.

Two of Diamonds

The two of diamonds relates to unexpected good news concerning financial matters. This news is likely to come from someone close to the client, and will bring pleasure to both. The sum of money involved will not be large, but will be welcome all the same. The client will be reaping this reward because of his or her abilities to deal with people in a harmonious way.

CLUBS

Section of medieval society: Peasants
Planet: Uranus
Element: Earth
Tarot card equivalent: Wands

The cards in the suit of clubs relate to creativity, enthusiasm, enterprise, and hard work. The clubs are ambitious, independent, and honest. The keyword is "enterprise."

Ace of Clubs

The ace of clubs is a powerful card that shows the client is ambitious, and has important hopes and dreams. However, he or she needs to channel these dreams into productive areas and then work hard to make them a reality. If the client is prepared to do this, success is inevitable.

If this card is one of the first three cards dealt in the spread, it is a sign that the client has been blessed with talents that are out of the ordinary. These talents can take him or her a long way. The client will be imaginative, intuitive, sensitive, and creative.

King of Clubs

The king of clubs is a man who knows much more than he lets on. He is affable and easy to get along with, but has a serious side to his nature. It takes time to get to know him well. This man has been hurt in the past and, as a consequence, has put up a protective barrier to shield himself from the criticisms of others. The king of clubs has many interests, some of which are solitary, as he enjoys time on his own. The king of clubs is sometimes lonely and is at his best inside a close, loving, understanding relationship.

If this card is one of the first three cards dealt in a spread for a male client, it is a sign that the card symbolizes him. If the card appears elsewhere in the spread, this card will represent someone the client knows.

If this card is one of the first three dealt in a female client's spread, it indicates a man who has a major role in her life.

Queen of Clubs

The queen of clubs is outwardly friendly, sociable, charming, and graceful, but inwardly she is shrewdly evaluating everything and manipulating the situation to her best advantage. She has good taste and enjoys being surrounded by beauty and luxury. She enjoys being the center of attention, but is subject to rapidly changing moods that sometimes drive people away. Consequently, she can be lonely and full of self-pity at times.

This card can symbolize a female client if it is one of the first three dealt in a spread. Alternatively, it can indicate some of the problems that this client is facing.

If this card is one of the first three dealt by a male client, it is a sign that a woman with these attributes will play a strong role in his life.

Jack of Clubs

The jack of clubs symbolizes a young person who is honest, reliable, hard-working, supportive, and sincere. This person, male or female, will be very fond of the client. Unfortunately, the client is likely to overlook this person, because he or she is content to remain in the background. However, the jack of clubs will ultimately prove to be a good friend who will remain, long after all the fair-weather friends have left.

The presence of this card anywhere in the spread is an indication that the client has a good friend of whom he or she is not truly aware. The client should learn to appreciate this person and not take him or her for granted.

Ten of Clubs

The ten of clubs relates to new beginnings. The client is likely to be planning new directions, but is reluctant to let go of the past. The new directions will mark a major change for the client, but his or her enthusiasm and energy will ensure that the efforts put in will pay off in time. This card frequently relates to confusion caused by the client's inability to separate his or her home and work lives.

Nine of Clubs

The nine of clubs represents feelings of satisfaction and contentment. The client will be achieving his or her goals and will be happy with the progress made so far. He or she will be particularly pleased that this success has come about without hurting others. The client will be starting to look for exciting new challenges that will stretch him or her further than ever before. The client will also enjoy working with, and being part of, group activities, often in a counseling or supportive role.

Eight of Clubs

The eight of clubs is a card of quiet happiness. The client will have learned many lessons, and will know that contentment and peace of mind come from small pleasures. In the past, material success will have been overemphasized, but this will be of much less importance in the future. No matter what happens in the client's life from now on, he or she will maintain a sense of inner peace and harmony.

If this card is one of the first three dealt in the spread, it is a sign that the client will be learning that true happiness can be lost if he or she overemphasizes work and money at the expense of what is really important in life.

Seven of Clubs

The seven of clubs is an indication that the client is better at starting things than at finishing them. It is a warning that the client needs to pay attention to the details, as otherwise his or her ventures could collapse. This card can sometimes indicate a dabbler, someone who flits from one thing to another, leaving behind a trail of half-finished projects. The client needs to spend time on his or her own to think, learn, and grow in knowledge and wisdom. In fact, he or she is likely to enjoy spending time on solitary or introspective activities. If the client is prepared to do this, the future will prove much more successful than the past.

The seven of clubs is often an indication of danger ahead. However, this danger can always be averted if the client is prepared to do the things that need to be done to ensure success.

Six of Clubs

The six of clubs is a sign that the client's social life will be improving. He or she will make valuable contacts that will prove helpful in every area of life. The client's own home and family life will be more agreeable than in the past, partly because the client will be more easy-going than he or she used to be, and will also be better at expressing his or her feelings. The client will have to ensure that his or her own needs are being met as this card shows a tendency toward self-sacrifice.

Five of Clubs

The five of clubs is a warning of a disagreement between two friends. This is likely to be caused when one of them progresses further or faster than the other. The warning is for the client to genuinely enjoy the successes of his or her friends, and not to flaunt his or her own successes in the faces of others. The client will be aware that he or she is versatile and can do anything that he or she wishes. Becoming jealous or upset about other people's achievements takes valuable time and energy that could be put to much more constructive use. Friendships are too important to allow petty disputes to end them.

Four of Clubs

The four of clubs is a welcoming card as it shows that the client will receive help from others whenever it is needed. The client works hard and is sometimes reluctant to ask others for help. This card shows that the client is a good friend who is probably not aware of the high esteem in which he or she is held by others. The client finds it hard to express his or her emotions.

Incidentally, in the past, card players considered the four of clubs to be the devil's card, and it was always a bad omen if this card appeared in the early stages of a game. Sometimes this card was known as the "devil's four-poster bed."

Three of Clubs

The three of clubs indicates temporary unpleasantness. The client might be the victim of a calculated snub, or some malicious gossip. The client may even accidentally cause the unpleasantness through his or her own actions. How the client responds to this will determine how serious it ultimately becomes. If he or she shows generosity and forgiveness, the slight will quickly be forgotten. The client will then be able to carry on enjoying life. If, on the other hand, he or she allows the matter to get out of proportion, it is likely to become a festering sore that hurts everyone.

Two of Clubs

The two of clubs is a card of potential. It shows that the client will receive an invitation that is of no immediate account, but will open doorways to new opportunities. The invitation is connected to either romance or career. The client will have an opportunity to demonstrate his or her intuition and people skills. The client is likely to be idealistic and overly modest, and hold back when he or she should be moving forward.

three

LEARNING
THE CARDS

Learning the meanings of all the cards can be a daunting process. Fifty-three different cards is a lot to memorize. Fortunately, there is a mnemonic system that will allow you to remember the keywords with just a little bit of practice.

THE SUITS

Each of the suits relates to a different area of interest. The hearts and the diamonds are the easiest to remember: the hearts relate to love and romance, and the diamonds relate to money.

Fortunately, the black cards are also easy to remember. The spades relate to changes of various sorts. Most people fear change, so the spades sometimes also serve as a warning. The clubs relate to creativity and hard work.

We can expand these keywords almost indefinitely:

Hearts relate to love, marriage, pleasure, laughter, companionship, joy, and happy times.

Diamonds relate to money, finance, business, prestige, success, and power.

Spades relate to change, unexpected happenings, confusion, mystery, challenges, warnings, and the unknown.

Clubs relate to creativity, energy, hard work, opportunities, and reward.

We can tell a great deal about a spread at a glance if one suit predominates. There is a famous tapestry in Scotland showing Mary Queen of Scots, and her adviser, David Rizzio, gazing in horror at the cards that had been dealt for her. The spread consisted of several spades and one heart. The warning of this spread came true. Rizzio was murdered, and Mary was imprisoned by her half-sister, Queen Elizabeth I, and eventually executed.

THE NUMBER CARDS

Each number has a meaning according to numerology.

One

Keyword: Independence

The number one relates to new beginnings. It is full of energy and enthusiasm. It relates to independence, new ideas, motivation, and energy. It also relates to ultimate attainment.

Two

Keyword: Cooperation

Number two relates to tact and cooperation. It is gentle, intuitive, kind, and caring. It is sensitive to the feelings of others. It is diplomatic, friendly, and loving.

Three

Keyword: Self-expression

Number three relates to communication and self-expression. It is lighthearted, frivolous, optimistic, and full of the joys of life. It is enthusiastic, but is better at starting projects than at finishing them. It is highly creative and expresses itself well.

Four

Keywords: Hard work

Number four relates to hard work, organization, and system and order. It represents the plodder who always gets the job done eventually. It often relates to feelings of limitation and restriction. Four is serious and rigid in outlook.

Five

Keywords: Constructive use of freedom

Number five relates to freedom, expansion, and variety. Five does not want to be restricted or confined in any way. It seeks excitement and remains forever young. Five is multitalented, and needs to learn how to use these talents wisely.

Six

Keyword: Responsibility

Number six relates to home and family matters. It is hard-working, responsible, loyal, and loving. Six can harmonize and balance difficult situations. Six is sympathetic, understanding, and appreciative.

Seven

Keyword: Learning

Seven relates to learning and growing in knowledge and wisdom. It is an introspective, spiritual number. Seven enjoys time on its own to reflect and meditate. The seven always has a unique, and frequently unconventional, approach to anything it does.

Eight

Keyword: Money

Number eight is a material number. It likes to be involved in large-scale enterprises. It relates to finance and money. It is inclined to be stubborn, single-minded, and rigid in outlook. Eight is conscious of status and needs to be successful to feel happy.

Nine

Keyword: Humanitarianism

Number nine is a humanitarian number. It is concerned with humanity in general, more than specific individuals. It is selfless, and enjoys giving. Nine's pleasure and satisfaction comes from giving.

Ten

Keyword: Attainment

There is no number ten in numerology, as ten is reduced down to a one (1 + 0 = 1). For card-reading purposes, consider the ten to be a slightly older, more mature, one.

Ten indicates the same new beginnings as a one, but is less brash and more cautious. It has similar energy to a one, but this energy is more controlled.

THE COURT CARDS

The court cards always relate to specific people in the client's life. Often it is the client, and in some spreads this card is deliberately inserted into the spread to depict the client.

Jacks

Jacks are usually young people of either sex. They are naïve, eager, and not entirely wise about the ways of the world. Sometimes the jack is about the same age as the client.

Queens

Queens are strong and often powerful women who are intimately connected with the client. In the case of a female client, the queen may represent her. In the case of a male client, the queen is usually the dominant female influence in his life.

Kings

Kings are usually mature men of influence and power. They are able to offer sound advice and counsel. A king can sometimes represent a male client. A king is a strong male figure in the life of a female client.

PUTTING IT TOGETHER

All you have to do now is to connect the number or court card to the suit. The three of diamonds relates to communication (three) about money (diamonds). Because the three also expresses the joys of life, this card could indicate spending money, or having fun talking about money.

How about the seven of clubs? This card relates to learning and spiritual growth (seven) and creativity and hard work (clubs). The client has the potential to work hard and learn something that relates to his or her creativity or spiritual growth. He or she may gain unique spiritual insights as a result.

The jack of hearts relates to a young or naïve person (jack) who is enjoying life and learning the excitement and pleasures of love (hearts).

The eight of diamonds is an interesting card as money is emphasized in both the number and suit. This gives the potential for enormous financial success. However, the client may have to learn from his or her mistakes. This is because he or she is likely to be rigid, stubborn, and even obstinate. However, you can guarantee that this person will persevere until he or she achieves worldly success, as the client will not feel truly happy until this occurs.

It can be a useful exercise to go through all the cards in the deck and interpret them with keywords. You will be surprised at just how quickly you learn all the basic meanings, especially if you use odd spare moments to practice. Once you can go through the entire deck of cards without hesitation, you will gradually be able to enlarge on the keywords. You can do this using the interpretations in chapter 2, and also by using your own intuition.

Some people find it helpful to write the keywords on each card. There is nothing wrong with this, and I have received readings from professional card readers who have used cards with words written on them. Anything that aids the learning process is good, but do not become reliant on using cards that are marked in this way. It takes time to learn the meanings of the cards, but once you have absorbed them, they will remain with you for life. When you reach this stage, you will be able to read cards anywhere, at any time, with any deck that happens to be available. If you rely on your own deck with the keywords written on them you will always be limited and restricted.

The more you practice, the better you will become. Ultimately, all you will need to do is glance at the spread of cards before weaving a fascinating, insightful, and relevant story about them. Once you reach this stage, you will be in a position to help people enormously with your new talent.

four

How to Interpret Groups of Cards

Once you know the meanings of the individual cards, you will be able to give good readings for others. However, these readings will become much more insightful and helpful once you discover the relationships that the different cards have to each other.

PREDOMINANCE OF COLORS AND SUITS

Naturally, when you deal out the cards you will immediately notice the colors and suits. This alone tells you a great deal.

In a spread of, say, fifteen cards, you would expect to have seven, eight, or nine cards of each color. However, you may find that almost all of the cards are one color. This means something.

If most of the cards are red, the outcome will be positive. If most of the cards are black, it means the client will be on something of a roller coaster ride, with plenty of ups and downs.

The same thing applies with the suits. A spread with a predominance of one suit in it has to be looked at carefully.

The spades have always been considered cards of mystery. Consequently, a predominance of spades in the spread indicates obstacles, confusion, changes, unexpected events, and the possibility of danger. The client needs to stay positive, think before speaking, and obtain expert advice before acting.

A predominance of hearts is usually a good thing as it indicates a time of laughter, happiness, and joy. Hearts are frequently an indication of success. However, if almost all the cards in the spread are hearts, it is a sign that the client will overindulge in various ways and have little or no concern for others.

A predominance of diamonds indicates important financial and business dealings, as well as the practical side of life. However, if most of the cards in the spread are diamonds, there is a risk that the client will become consumed by his or her drive for money, and will think about nothing else.

A predominance of clubs indicates a varied, interesting, and stimulating period ahead. The client will make the most of new opportunities, and will make new friends. In fact, friendship is one of the strongest aspects of the clubs. They emphasize the need for friends, and how we need to be a friend to make friends. If most of the cards in the spread are clubs, the client will be tempted to take on much more than he or she can reasonably handle.

PREDOMINANCE OF HIGH AND LOW CARDS

If most of the cards in the spread are high ones, especially aces and court cards, it is a sign that the client is about to experience major changes in his or her life. These changes are likely to be important and influence the client's future.

The opposite applies if most of the cards are low in value. This is a sign that the client's life will continue along the same lines as before. He or she is not ready yet for any major decisions or changes.

CARD COMBINATIONS

The presence of two, three, or four of a kind modifies the reading. The cards do not need to be next to each other, and can be located anywhere in the spread. A pair of cards—two aces, for example—does not have great significance. However, it means that these cards should be looked at closely, and will be more important than usual. Three or four cards of the same value affect the reading greatly.

Aces

Three aces indicates new opportunities and dynamic action. The client will have the necessary enthusiasm and energy to make it happen.

Four aces indicates the potential for success in every area of life. The client's abilities will be at their peak and he or she will feel confident of achieving any goal. Four aces can also mean that the client is about to achieve success after a great deal of hard work and effort.

Kings

For male clients, three kings indicates useful contacts and good support from others. For female clients this indicates more male friends, the possibility of romance, and a busy social life.

For male clients, four kings indicates greater responsibilities, respect, and admiration from others, and an increase in self-esteem. For female clients this indicates relationships with men, and the possibility of jealousy and backstabbing.

Queens

Three queens indicates new friendships with women. These acquaintances have the potential to be important in the future, and the client will have to move forward slowly and with caution, as these women will have hidden depths and be hard to assess at a glance.

Four queens for a male client indicates that he may be caught up in an embarrassing or compromising situation. For a female client this is an indication that other women are watching her closely and talking about her behind her back.

Jacks

Three jacks is a sign of a disagreement. The client will have to step in and calm things down before it grows out of proportion.

Four jacks is a sign of quarrels and arguments, usually involving young people.

Tens

Three tens is a sign of financial improvement. Someone may repay a loan, or the client may receive a small windfall.

Four tens indicates a change for the better. A stage of life is now over and the client will be starting again with new enthusiasm.

Nines

Three nines is a sign of happiness and fulfillment. This is usually unexpected and is the result of a change in attitude, either by the client or by people close to him or her.

Four nines indicates a period of success and good fortune. The client will have to enjoy his or her success quietly, as the achievements will not be recognized or appreciated by others.

Eights

Three eights is a sign that financial pressures are easing. Something that the client does improves his or her finances.

Four eights is an indication of financial worries and business problems. These difficulties seem important at the time, but pass quickly.

Sevens

Three sevens is a sign of a temporary setback. The client should ignore the comments and opinions of others, and keep his or her eyes firmly on the ultimate goal.

Four sevens indicates that the client will feel totally alone and isolated. He or she should use this time to clarify what is going on in his or her life, and to decide where to go from here.

Sixes

Three sixes is an indication of new opportunities that are presented by people close to the client.

Four sixes indicates a pleasant delay. Home and family matters will temporarily distract the client from his or her goals, but will prove enjoyable and worthwhile.

Fives

Three fives is potentially dangerous. The client is likely to feel restricted in some way and will be tempted to do something to escape. He or she needs to think carefully before acting.

Four fives means that the client has a number of decisions to make. It will be difficult for him or her to choose, purely because of the large number of choices involved.

Fours

Three fours indicates some major obstacle has been overcome. The client should pause, relax, and enjoy him- or herself before starting work again.

Four fours shows that the client is seeking a worth-while challenge. This is likely to be several steps beyond anything he or she has attempted before. The client should think hard, work out a plan, and then seize the opportunity.

Threes

Three threes is a warning to the client to avoid idle gossip. The client should not believe everything he or she hears.

Four threes indicates a large amount of communication. The client will have to synthesize a huge amount of information and decide what is factual and what is not.

Twos

Three twos gives the client pleasant, happy times with close friends and loved ones. It also provides an opportunity to share ideas with people the client respects and admires.

Four twos shows that the client is likely to be overly sensitive about something someone says or does. The client should keep his own counsel, and not respond until he or she has thought the matter through.

OTHER SIGNIFICANT COMBINATIONS

Whenever an ace appears in a spread, it is a good idea to look at the cards surrounding it, as they frequently affect the interpretation.

Ace of Diamonds

If the ace of diamonds is surrounded by several hearts, it is a warning that the client must not mix business and pleasure. He or she will be able to do one or the other, but will lose both if he or she tries to mix them.

If the ace of diamonds is surrounded by several spades, it is a sign of financial disruption. The client needs to consolidate, act cautiously, and wait for the upheaval to end. The tendency in this sort of situation is to panic. Acting in this way will lead to major losses.

If the ace of diamonds is surrounded by several clubs, it is a sign that hard work will pay off financially.

Ace of Spades

If the ace of spades is surrounded by several hearts, it is a sign of emotional ups and downs. The client should take a step back and look at the situation dispassionately.

If the ace of spades is surrounded by several diamonds, it is a sign of financial ups and downs. The client should conserve money when it is plentiful to sustain him or her in the leaner times.

If the ace of spades is surrounded by several clubs, it is a sign that although the client will be working hard, he or she will still experience ups and downs in his or her career.

Ace of Hearts

If the ace of hearts is surrounded by several clubs, it is a sign that the client's generous nature will be recognized and appreciated by others.

If the ace of hearts is surrounded by several diamonds, it is a sign of love, travel, and money.

If the ace of hearts is surrounded by several spades, it is a sign of ups and downs in the client's love life.

Ace of Clubs

If the ace of clubs is surrounded by several diamonds, it is a sign of increased wealth and position.

If the ace of clubs is surrounded by several spades, it is a sign of financial difficulties.

If the ace of clubs is surrounded by several hearts, it is a sign of love, romance, good fortune, and happiness.

Court Cards

A large number of court cards in the spread indicates a party or large-scale social event. It is a time for feasting and celebration.

If a jack is found next to a king or queen, it is a sign that the client is being protected.

If a jack is surrounded by several diamonds, it is a sign of good news from afar.

If the queen of spades is found between any two other court cards, it is a sign of malicious gossip.

If the queen of spades is found between another queen and a king, it is a sign of a relationship breakup.

CARDS FLANKED BY TWO CARDS OF THE SAME SUIT

Any card that is flanked by two cards from the same suit takes on many of the traits of that suit. This can be good or bad. For example, if the two of hearts (quiet pleasures inside a love relationship) is flanked by two spades, the time these two people spend together is likely to be discordant rather than pleasant.

On the other hand, if the five of spades (card of tears) is flanked by two clubs, the adverse effects are softened enormously by the friendship and support of the two clubs.

five

HOW TO READ YOUR OWN CARDS

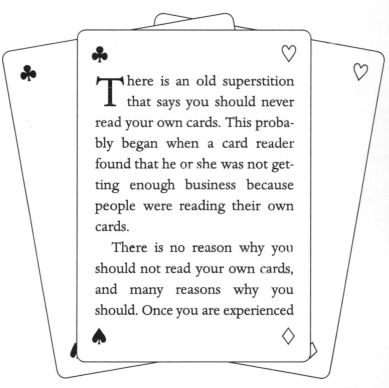

There is an old superstition that says you should never read your own cards. This probably began when a card reader found that he or she was not getting enough business because people were reading their own cards.

There is no reason why you should not read your own cards, and many reasons why you should. Once you are experienced at reading cards, you will find that the readings you give yourself will help you in every area of your life. The cards will guide and direct you, provide warnings of dangers ahead, and provide clues as to future directions.

There are advantages and disadvantages of reading your own cards. Naturally, you know yourself better than anyone else. Consequently, you will be able to discern all sorts of information that might escape someone else who is simply reading the cards. The disadvantage, of course, is that you might be tempted to misread the information to make the cards fit what you want to have happen, rather than what the future will be. Whenever I feel that I might be tempted to misinterpret the reading, I ask someone else to do it for me. Naturally, I do not read my own cards if I have an emotional involvement in the outcome, or am under stress. However, at all other times, I read the cards for myself.

I am also happy to read cards for members of my family, except when I feel that I am too emotionally involved in the outcome to give a good reading. Readings for members of your family can be helpful for everyone. Frequently, information that I see in my son's cards, for instance, may be further clarified in my daughter's cards. The interplay of information between each member of the family enables you to build up a complete picture that would not be known otherwise.

It can be difficult to develop the necessary detachment to read your own cards and those of close members of your family, but it is a skill well worth developing.

I believe that the future can be changed. If the cards reveal an outcome that you do not want, you have the power to change it. It is not easy, but it can be done. You may have to look at things differently, and change various things in your life, but because you have the power of choice and free will, you can make anything of your life that you wish. The cards will help to guide you in the right direction.

Although the cards can be extremely useful to you in providing help and guidance, you should not depend solely on them. Read the cards, by all means, but also think about the situation, ask others for help, and seek professional advice when necessary.

I have met people who read their own cards one or more times a day. This is probably a good idea for someone who is learning the cards as the practice will be beneficial, but it is not a good habit to get into. Reading the cards once a week should be enough.

It is a good idea to write down the questions you intend on asking the cards as far in advance as possible. This allows your subconscious mind to start working on the problem well before you cast the cards.

Think about just one of your questions while shuffling the cards. A single spread might answer more than one of your questions, but most of the time you will have to create new spreads for each question.

CHOOSING YOUR SIGNIFICATOR CARD

Choose a card to represent you using the guidelines for choosing a significator card in chapter 1. The description does not need to be 100 percent accurate. If you have brown hair and gray eyes, you could choose a club or a heart to symbolize you. There is no need to agonize over your choice. It is simply a symbol of you to place in the center of the spread.

In fact, one reader I know chooses the significator card by chance. If the client is male, she has him mix the four kings together facedown, and then take one of them to act as his significator. Naturally, she uses the four queens when reading for a woman.

A SAMPLE SPREAD

Let's assume that you are going to create a spread for yourself. Your question is, "Will my finances improve over the next three months?" You may or may not start with a prayer asking for protection and guidance. This is entirely up to you. Many card readers pray at the start and the end of their readings, but just as many do not.

First of all, you need to locate the card that describes you. Place this card in the center of the table, and then shuffle the cards. (For the purposes of this sample reading, we will assume that the jack of diamonds is the card that represents you.) Think about your question while mixing the cards and dealing them out (Figure 2). The first two cards are placed on each side of the jack of diamonds. They are the queen of hearts and the ace of hearts. The next three cards (the past) are the ten of clubs in the middle, flanked by the nine of hearts and the four of hearts. The next three cards reveal the factors that are out of your control. They are the eight of spades, flanked by the four of clubs and two of spades. You then deal out three cards to represent the course of your life if you make no changes. They are the queen of diamonds, flanked by the jack of hearts and the six of diamonds. Finally, you deal out the three cards that represent the future—the ten of diamonds, flanked by the ace of spades and the five of diamonds.

The first thing you notice is that the spread contains ten red cards and five black cards. This is positive. No one suit predominates, though there are five hearts. This means the next three months (the period of time covered by the question) will be happy.

Ten of the fifteen cards are high cards (eight or above). This means that you will be experiencing changes in the next three months.

The spread contains two aces, two queens, two tens, and two fours. This is a good balance. The only other factors that can be seen at a glance are the ten of clubs

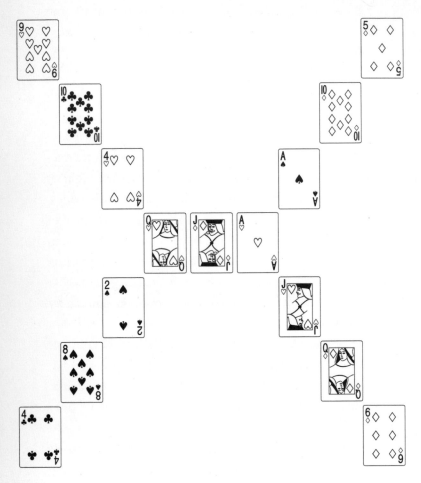

Figure 2
Sample reading.

flanked by two hearts, and the jack of hearts beside the queen of diamonds. The ten of clubs relates to new beginnings. The two hearts could indicate that this new start relates to a love relationship. However, as the question is about money rather than romance, it is more likely to indicate that you will have had the support of close, loving friends. As it is in the row of the past, you will know what it is. The jack of hearts next to the queen of diamonds indicates protection.

With practice, you will notice these things at a glance. Now it is time to look at the individual cards. You start with the first three cards dealt, the row that indicates the present. Two of them are hearts, indicating a pleasant, harmonious present. The jack of diamonds represents you. The queen of hearts gains added importance beside another court card. If you are female, it is a sign that you already have many of the qualities of this queen. If you are male, it shows that you are loved. The ace of hearts is also an important card, showing joy, happiness, and contentment. This card, plus the queen of hearts, could indicate a stable, close, happy family life.

Now it is time to look to the past. We have already partially covered this. The ten of clubs flanked by two hearts indicates a new start with the blessing and support of loved ones. The nine of hearts is the happiest card in the entire deck, while the four of hearts indicates satisfaction and pleasure from helping others.

The past and the present look happy and contented, but so far we have not encountered a single diamond to signify money. The next diagonal row does not provide any either. This row denotes factors that are out of your control. The principal card is the eight of spades, the happiest card in this suit. On its right is the two of spades, which indicates a temporary inconvenience. The four of clubs shows that you will receive any help necessary at this time. There is nothing to worry about in this row.

The next two rows show your two choices. You can carry on with your life in exactly the way you are now, which is revealed by the bottom diagonal row to the right of the spread, or you can make some changes and pursue the path shown in the upper diagonal row.

First, in the row that shows the outcome if you make no changes, we finally have some money cards. The central card of this row is the queen of diamonds. This indicates a strong, powerful woman who will motivate and inspire you. To her right is the six of diamonds. This is a money card, but there is a price to be paid. You will have to leave your loving, stable, happy family and go out into the world to seek the relatively modest financial rewards that this card promises. The jack of hearts provides protection (as it is next to a queen). For the purposes of this reading, this card indicates the potential of a pleasant break from the normal day-to-day routine. It looks as if the future is agreeably pleasant if you carry on the way you are now. Your fortunes will improve slowly, but will involve periods away from home.

Finally, we look at the future that you can create for yourself. In the center of this final row is the ten of diamonds, not exactly the card we would have wished for, considering the nature of the question. This card means that you are paying too much attention to the financial side of life, and are likely to be bored with the current situation. To the right of this card is the five of diamonds, which indicates a difference of opinion concerning money. However, it can also indicate a sudden change in your fortunes. The last card in this row is the ace of spades, the most powerful card in the deck of cards. This gives you enthusiasm, energy, and enormous power, but it has to be used wisely. This card indicates major changes that will work out well if your motives are good. It appears that if you follow this road, there will be disagreements about money, but also the potential for huge financial gain. There will be risks involved in following this path. However, as it looks as if you are bored with the status quo (ten of diamonds) this might be the path to follow. Naturally, the final decision is up to you.

JUDELLE'S READING

Here is another example. A close relative of mine asked the cards if her relationship with her current boyfriend would develop further. He had been transferred to another city and Judelle was concerned that the relationship might gradually fade away to nothing. Judelle chose the jack of hearts as her significator. When she dealt the cards, almost all of them were hearts (Figure 3). This was positive as it indicates laughter, happiness, and fun. However, when almost all the cards in a spread are hearts, it is an indication that Judelle will be tempted to overindulge in various ways and think only of herself.

The cards that flanked the jack of hearts were the ten and three of hearts. These indicate the current situation and give an accurate picture of what is going on in Judelle's life. The ten of hearts indicates good news. This is likely to be the promotion and pay raise her boyfriend received. This is excellent news, as they ultimately intend to get married. However, the three of hearts is a sign of setbacks and disappointments. This could mean the young couple's forced separation, which is proving difficult for both of them.

The row that symbolizes the past contained the four of hearts, flanked by the queen of hearts and the four of diamonds. The queen of hearts possibly represents Judelle, as it indicates someone who is lighthearted, carefree, and emotional—all qualities that she possesses

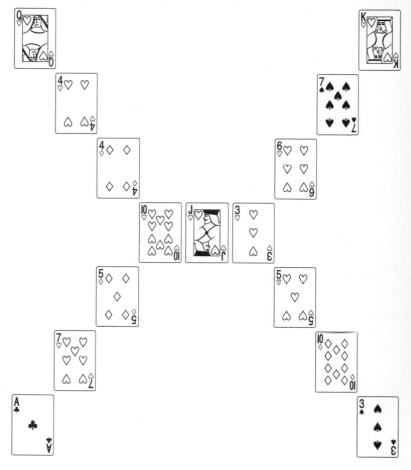

Figure 3
Judelle's reading.

in full measure. However, these qualities are also present in her mother. Judelle felt her mother had little influence on her, but the presence of the queen of hearts here could well indicate that she is a stronger force in Judelle's life than she realizes. The four of hearts indicates happiness gained from helping others. Judelle works as a nurse, and she loves her job. The four of diamonds is a sign of money gained through hard work and good money management. It is a standing joke in the family that once Judelle has money, it is carefully invested. She is not frugal, but is careful with money, and looks after it well.

The next row relates to factors that are out of Judelle's control. Here we had the seven of hearts, flanked by the ace of clubs and the five of diamonds. This is an interesting selection of cards, and shows that more is going on under the surface than Judelle realized. The ace of clubs denotes ambition. Judelle is determined to be successful in life. She is single-minded, and enjoys setting goals and working toward them. The seven of hearts is a sign of a disagreement. It traditionally denotes a lover's quarrel. The five of diamonds gives a hint as to what the disagreement is about, as it indicates differing opinions about money. Her boyfriend is placid and easygoing, while she is goal-oriented and ambitious. It is easy to see how financial problems could affect their relationship.

Now we look at the outcome if no changes are made. In this row we had the ten of diamonds, flanked by the five of hearts and the three of spades. These cards provide a strong warning. The five of hearts is an indication of a major change, and usually marks the end of a relationship. The three of spades depicts some form of sudden or unexpected communication. The ten of diamonds shows that Judelle pays too much attention to the material side of life. She wants her and her partner to enjoy a secure financial start in life, unaware that this is actually threatening to end the relationship. If she doesn't do something about this, the relationship will end suddenly, probably with bad feelings on both sides.

Finally, we look at the cards that represent the future that she and her boyfriend can create for themselves. This row shows the seven of spades, flanked by the six of hearts and the king of hearts. The king of hearts represents her boyfriend, and is a strong indication that the relationship can be made to work, with love and understanding on both sides. The person depicted by the king of hearts finds it hard to express his innermost feelings, and Judelle will have to work at encouraging him to express himself more freely. The six of hearts is a sign of slow, steady progress. It indicates that Judelle should be more patient. Finally, the seven of spades is a sign of partial success, but with the potential for long-term success if Judelle is prepared to work at it.

This reading alerted Judelle to problems she was not aware of, and enabled her to make the necessary changes before the difficulties began. She and her boyfriend are now engaged, and plan to get married in the next twelve months.

Can you see how helpful a reading of this sort can be? Once you have this information, you are in a much stronger position to decide on your course of action. You will be in control of your own destiny. You will know when to forge ahead, and when to pause and wait. You will be forewarned against dangers and other pitfalls. You will also become more aware of opportunities and be able to take advantage of them. The cards can become a valuable guide to every area of your life.

You can probably also see why you should not try to read your own cards when the outcome affects you emotionally, or you are upset or under enormous stress. "Will my fortunes improve in the next three months?" is a completely different type of question than "Should I get a divorce?" With questions like the latter, it is definitely better to have someone else read the cards for you.

In the next chapter we will start reading the cards for someone else.

six

How to Read the Cards for Others

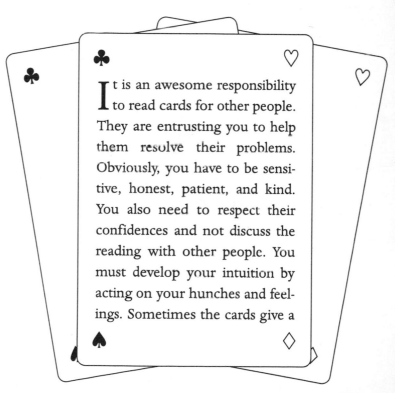

It is an awesome responsibility to read cards for other people. They are entrusting you to help them resolve their problems. Obviously, you have to be sensitive, honest, patient, and kind. You also need to respect their confidences and not discuss the reading with other people. You must develop your intuition by acting on your hunches and feelings. Sometimes the cards give a vague impression or a general meaning that becomes clear only when you use your intuition.

Your clients will come to you because they have problems in their lives and need help. Your skills with the cards will enable them to see their difficulties in a new light. However, you must never tell the client what to do. The client needs to decide on the correct course of action for him- or herself. You can provide insight into the problems the client is facing. In the process, you will frequently come up with suggested plans of action. Most of the time, the client will know what he or she should be doing, and will have come to you for confirmation. The cards will clarify matters and provide hope that there is a solution.

As a fortune-teller you have a duty to remain as positive as possible. Look for the good things in the cards, rather than the negative. Naturally, you will have to explain the negative things you see, but stress the positive.

A SAMPLE READING

Raymond is a twenty-one-year-old man who has just finished college and is looking for his first job. He has a liberal arts degree, and is not sure for what type of job to aim. He has been told about an entry-level position in a television station and came to me because he was not sure if he should apply for it. He is a good-looking young man with an athletic build. His tanned face showed that he enjoyed being outdoors. It was obvious to me that his significator card was the jack of hearts.

After placing this card on the table, I gave him the cards to mix. He shuffled them thoroughly while composing his question.

"Should I apply for this job, and if I do, would I get it?" He laughed nervously. "That's sort of two questions. Can I ask that?"

I nodded. "Sure. Both questions are connected. Let's see what the cards have to say about it."

Raymond watched closely as I dealt the cards (Figure 4). "Eight red cards," he said when I finished.

I looked at him curiously. He had not mentioned any knowledge about divination with playing cards. "What does that mean?" I asked.

Raymond licked his lips and looked embarrassed. "My Mum does the cards sometimes. Not like this; she deals them out in a straight line. If there are more reds than blacks the outcome is good."

I nodded. "That's right. It also means the near future will be happy. Have you noticed that nine of the cards are eight or above? That means you'll be experiencing some changes."

"Are they good or bad?"

"We'll see. Now, these three cards in the center indicate the present. That's you in the middle. The seven of clubs here shows that you are better at starting things than you are at finishing them."

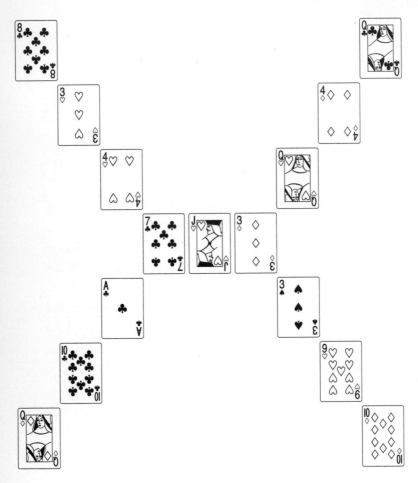

Figure 4
Raymond's reading.

Raymond grinned. "I'm a dreamer. Everyone tells me that."

I touched the three of diamonds. "This card relates to talking about money. It sometimes means contracts and legal papers."

Raymond shook his head. "I'm always talking about money, but that's only 'cause I don't have any. I've never had anything to do with contracts."

"If you put these three cards together it looks as if you daydream about your need for money."

Raymond's eyes widened. "That sounds just like me."

"Let's see what is behind you, the past. In the center is the three of hearts."

"Love. Hearts mean love."

I nodded. "That's right. In this case it relates to disappointment about love."

Raymond nodded. "My fault."

"Next to it is the eight of clubs. It's a sign of happiness. There might have been disappointments in love, but basically it was a happy time, especially as you also have the four of hearts. That indicates pleasures gained through helping others."

Raymond nodded. "Does that include animals? I wanted to work with animals when I was a kid."

"Yes, this card emphasizes all living things—people, animals, plants. Now, this row shows the things that you can't change. These are out of your control."

Raymond looked at them with interest. "A queen and an ace. It can't be too bad."

"It's not bad at all. The middle card is the ten of clubs. It relates to your question. It represents new starts, but a reluctance to move ahead. Part of you is clinging to the past."

"I enjoyed college. It's a bit scary leaving that behind, especially when you have a useless degree like mine."

I shook my head. "It's not useless, Raymond. All education is valuable, and your degree shows a prospective employer that you are capable of setting goals and working hard."

"Not a degree like mine."

"If you feel like that, why did you spend the last three years working hard to get it?"

Raymond shrugged his shoulders. "I didn't know what I wanted. I thought teaching might be a good career for me, but I've gone right off that idea. The trouble is, I don't really know what I want."

"There's a strong woman here, the queen of diamonds. She's passionate, fiery even. She has a good brain and can run rings around anyone."

"My mother. You're right, I can't do anything about her."

"And finally in this row, the ace of clubs. It's an extremely good card. It shows that you have hopes and dreams. You told me you're a daydreamer, but this is much more than that. If you learn how to channel those dreams in constructive directions, you'll go a long, long way."

Raymond's face expressed doubt.

"Now we have two rows representing the future. This row shows what will happen if you carry on much the way you are now. The other row shows what will happen if you make certain changes, and move forwards. First, the row that shows what will happen if you do nothing. If you don't apply for this job, say. The nine of hearts in the middle is a supremely happy and contented card. However, this is likely to be affected by the three of spades. This shows that you are likely to act without thinking, and somehow rock the boat. The ten of diamonds indicates boredom. You want to escape, but don't know how to do it. You are getting ready to enter the material world, and think of it all the time. At the same time, though, part of you rejects it. If you follow this path, you will be happy, but confused and frustrated."

Raymond laughed. "That describes the situation right now."

"I'm not surprised. Now, let's see what happens if you do apply for the job. We have the four of diamonds in the middle. That is the card of slow, steady progress. Your fortunes will improve slowly. You have the queen of hearts beside it. That's a sign of a lighthearted, carefree, intuitive woman in your life. She obviously has something to do with your question."

Raymond nodded. "That'll be my sister. She's the one who saw the ad in the paper. She wants me to apply for it."

"You are fortunate in having a sister like her. Finally we have the queen of clubs. You have three strong women around you. This woman is friendly and easy to get on with. Inwardly, though, she is shrewd, calculating, and good at business." I looked at Raymond. "Any idea who she might be?"

He shook his head.

"It's probably your boss, as this woman has an important part to play in your immediate future."

"Would I get the job?"

I nodded. "It seems extremely likely to me, with these three cards. However, it will only happen if you apply for the position." I indicated the previous row. "Of course, if you don't apply for this, or other positions, your future will be happy, but rather boring and unfulfilled."

The television station took Raymond on as a trainee. He phoned to tell me about it.

"It all came true except for that queen at the end," he said. "My boss is a man. There are lots of women here, but I don't have much to do with any of them."

Two weeks later he called again to tell me that his boss had been promoted, and he was now working for a woman who sounded just like the queen of clubs.

This reading shows how readings generally take the form of a conversation. Of course, people vary enormously. I have given many readings where the client talks more than I do. I have also done readings where the client did not say a single word. I try to discourage this though. The reading is not intended to be a bravura display of the reader's psychic abilities. It is intended to clarify the client's problems and to provide possible answers to questions that have been causing concern.

ANOTHER READING

While working on this book, a middle-aged lady asked me for a reading. Virginia was an acquaintance of a friend who had asked me to do the reading as Virginia was going through a bad time. Virginia had never had a reading before, and was visibly nervous. She was dressed entirely in black and avoided making eye contact with me. She looked like a widow, and I guessed that she was in her early fifties.

I selected the queen of clubs as her significator, and then handed her the cards to mix.

"Think of a question you would like to have answered while you mix them," I said. "It would be helpful to tell me what the question is, but you don't have to if you don't want to."

Virginia shuffled the cards so proficiently that I asked her if she played cards. Virginia smiled slightly, and quietly said, "Yes." A card almost fell out of the deck as she stopped mixing them, but she caught it and pushed it back into the deck.

I took the cards from her, and dealt the first two cards on either side of the queen of clubs. They were the three of hearts and the joker (Figure 5).

"These cards indicate the present," I said. "The queen in the middle represents you, of course. The three of hearts relates to disappointment of some sort, usually in love. The joker is interesting as it shows that you are following your own path in life. It makes you unconventional, mysterious even. You are probably on a more spiritual path now than you used to be."

I glanced at Virginia as I spoke. She made no comments on what I had said, but asked, "Do you want to know my question?"

"Only if you want to tell me."

"Okay." Virginia crossed her arms and pursed her lips. She sat back in her chair. I could see that this reading was not going to be an easy one.

I quickly dealt out the other cards, telling Virginia which area of life each set of cards indicated as I placed them on the table.

Once the cards had been dealt, I looked at the spread to see what clues the cards could give me. There were nine red cards, compared to five black. This was a positive start. Apart from the joker, which always indicates an interesting reading, none of the cards provided immediate information.

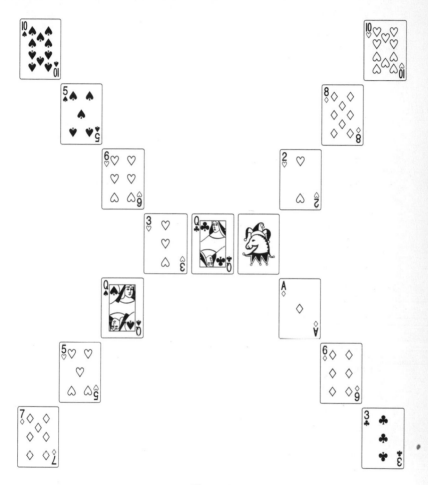

Figure 5
Virginia's reading.

"Well, you chose an interesting selection of cards," I said. "We've looked at the present. Let's look at these three cards first. They indicate the past. In the center is the five of spades. Traditionally, that is the card of tears, so you have obviously been through a difficult time. Next to it is the ten of spades, which indicates a blockage of some sort. It means that you have reached a dead end. You've probably had a major re-evaluation of some sort. The other card is the six of hearts, which is more positive, as it indicates a gradual improvement in your circumstances, although it also indicates that enormous patience is required. The two spades and the heart tend to indicate that the problems in the past relate to love."

Virginia gave no indication that she had even heard what I said. She was looking at the cards with what seemed to be mild curiosity.

"This group here represents things you cannot change. The three cards are the five of hearts, flanked by the seven of diamonds and the queen of spades. The five of hearts always relates to a major change, and, being a heart, this is probably to do with a relationship. It means that whatever it was came to an end. There was also a great deal of confusion, indicated by the seven of diamonds. For a while, your life was on hold, and you were unable to do anything. The queen of spades indicates a strong woman, possibly someone you were able to go to for advice."

"Mother." The word was said so quietly that I almost did not hear it. Virginia continued to stare blankly at the cards.

"Now we come to the two strands that represent the future. This one here," I said, indicating the right-hand row that headed downward to the right, "is your future, if you carry on exactly the way you are now. The other row shows what will occur if you make some important changes. First, we'll look at what the outcome will be if you carry on the way you are now. We have the six of diamonds, with the ace of diamonds and the three of clubs. That's an interesting mix. The six of diamonds shows that you will enjoy a pleasant home life, with a great deal of family security. The ace of diamonds is a sign of money coming in, which tends to reinforce the financial aspects of the six of diamonds. However, the three of clubs is a sign of some unpleasantness that will grow and fester unless you do something to eliminate it. This probably comes down to forgiveness."

I realized that Virginia was no longer looking at the cards, and was staring at me, her eyes narrowed. When I met her gaze, she looked back at the cards.

"What about the future if I make some changes?" she asked.

"That's much more positive," I replied. "The cards are all red—the eight of diamonds, flanked by the two and ten of hearts. The eight of diamonds is an indication of financial success, and also gives you a balanced approach to life. It is extremely positive, especially when accompanied by the two hearts. The two of hearts is a sign of a quiet, gentle relationship that builds and grows. You will enjoy pleasant, happy times together. The ten of hearts is a sign of good news. It will be unexpected, even though it will somehow be instigated by you." I tapped the last three cards. "If you are prepared to make some changes in your life, it looks as if you have a secure, happy future ahead of you."

Virginia nodded her head and gave a deep sigh.

"All right," she said. "What was my question?"

I shook my head. "Really, I don't care what your question was, as the cards tell me everything I need to know. However, looking at this spread, I'd say that you've obviously been through a bad time emotionally. It looks as if an important relationship has ended, and you're wondering if there is someone special in your future. These final three cards show that there is, and that you have a great deal of happiness ahead of you."

Virginia nodded again, smiled slightly, and stood up. "Interesting," she said. "Very interesting."

She left without saying another word. I was rather put out, as I dislike giving readings in which there is no input whatsoever from the other person. I always feel, rightly or wrongly, that these people are skeptical about card reading, and are simply testing me. Also, as I had done this reading purely as a favor for a friend, I expected a slight bit of gratitude. Consequently, I felt slightly annoyed, as I put the cards away and carried on with my day.

A few hours later, my friend phoned and told me how thrilled Virginia had been with her reading. She had wanted to know if she'd get married again, and I had answered the question perfectly. It was good to have this feedback, but I couldn't help feeling that Virginia would have received a much better reading if she had allowed it to become a conversation, rather than a monologue.

Frequently, your clients will not want or need a complete reading. In the next two chapters we will look at some spreads that can be done quickly and easily. They do not provide the amount of detail that the spread we have already learned provides, but they have the advantage of providing instant answers.

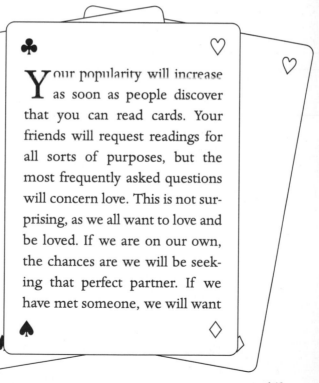

seven

LOVE AND ROMANCE

Your popularity will increase as soon as people discover that you can read cards. Your friends will request readings for all sorts of purposes, but the most frequently asked questions will concern love. This is not surprising, as we all want to love and be loved. If we are on our own, the chances are we will be seeking that perfect partner. If we have met someone, we will want to know if the relationship will develop and become permanent. Even inside a relationship, we will want confirmation that it will last and be happy.

Card readings can tell us if upcoming relationships will be good or bad. They can forewarn us about people who are not what they appear to be. They can help us recognize good qualities in people we may have overlooked. Naturally, we all want to know about happiness in the future, but card readings are just as valuable when they warn us about difficult relationships before we become deeply involved.

You can use the spread we have already learned to answer questions relating to love and romance. There are also special spreads that have been devised purely for this purpose.

LUCKY THREE

The nine of hearts has always been considered a lucky card. It is often called the "wish card." We use this card, plus the card that represents you, to determine your love life in the near future. (To refresh your memory, the suit of spades symbolizes people with dark hair and dark eyes. A woman would choose the queen of spades, and a man the king. A young person of either sex would choose the jack. The suit of clubs symbolizes people with brown hair and brown eyes. The suit of hearts symbolizes people with light brown hair and gray or blue eyes. The suit of diamonds symbolizes people with blonde or red hair.)

Thoroughly shuffle the cards and place them on the table. Cut about a third of the cards from the deck and place them on the table on the left-hand side of the stack. Take about half of the remaining cards from the deck and place them on the right-hand side. This creates three piles, each containing approximately one-third of the deck.

Pick up the cards in the left-hand pile and look through them. If both the nine of hearts and the card that symbolizes you are in this pile, you will meet your future partner in the near future.

If these two cards are not in the first pile, look at the second pile. If both cards are amongst these cards, you will meet your lover in the next twelve months.

If the nine of hearts and the card depicting you are found in the last pile, it is a sign that your lover is still a long way away and it will take more than a year for the two of you to find each other.

It is possible that the cards will not be in the same pile. If they are in piles that are next to each other, you will meet your lover, but it will take longer than you would like. If the two cards are found in the first and third piles, you will experience a number of relationships before finding the right person for you.

Several years ago, I demonstrated this technique at a party. One of the guests was extremely skeptical about card divination, and turned down the offer of having her cards read. Two years later, she phoned me to tell me that the Lucky Three method worked. As soon as she got home from the party, she went through this exercise and found both cards in the second pile. She forgot all about it, until she met the man of her dreams nine months later.

ADVICE FROM THE KINGS

Women have been seeking advice from a king on matters of the heart for hundreds of years. As well as a pack of cards, you will need two dice.

Shuffle the cards thoroughly. Hold the cards faceup and deal them one at a time into a pile on the table until the first king appears. Place this king on the table, and continue dealing cards until the second king appears. This is placed to the right of the first king. The third king is placed below the first king, and the fourth king is placed to his right, creating a square of four kings. The rest of the cards are put away.

Mix the dice together and toss them onto the table. The die that has the higher number on top is the one that will be used for the rest of the procedure. If both dice have the same number on top, they are tossed again. If they again produce a pair of numbers, it is an indication that the cards do not want to answer any questions today, and you will have to try again tomorrow.

We will assume that one of the dice had a higher number on top than the other one. Kiss the die gently to wish it luck. The die is now held about a foot above the four kings and dropped. The king that it lands on will provide the answer.

If the die lands with an odd number uppermost, the die is dropped again. You also need to drop the die again if it rolls and does not rest on any of the kings. You need to continue doing this until the die rests on one of the kings with a two, four, or six facing upward.

The answer is then interpreted (see below). After receiving an answer, you should not seek advice from the four kings for at least a month.

King of Spades

If the die rests on this card with the two-spot uppermost, you should pay no attention to the flattery of a tall, fair-haired man.

If the die rests on this card with the four-spot uppermost, you can expect an interesting proposal from an old friend.

If the die rests on this card with a six-spot uppermost, you will be tempted into a relationship that will cause grief.

King of Diamonds

If the die rests on this card with the two-spot uppermost, you must be extremely cautious. Relationships are likely to prove difficult in the near future.

If the die rests on this card with a four-spot uppermost, you can expect a wealthy suitor. He will be considerate, gentle, and kind, but be unable to express any of his deeper feelings.

If the die rests on this card with a six-spot uppermost, you will have to choose between two men. Making this decision will be difficult.

King of Hearts

If the die rests on this card with a two-spot uppermost, it is a sign of a short-lived romance with a dark-complexioned man.

If the die rests on this card with a four-spot uppermost, you will enjoy good times with a fun-loving man, until you discover his darker side.

If the die rests on this card with a six-spot uppermost, you will shortly meet a young man who will be charming, affectionate, and fun-loving.

King of Clubs

If the die rests on this card with a two-spot uppermost, you will be tempted to marry a young man who appears to have good prospects. Think carefully, as this is likely to be a bad move.

If the die rests on this card with a four-spot uppermost, you will put your faith and trust in a young man who does not deserve it.

If the die rests on this card with a six-spot uppermost, you will shortly meet a young man who has much more potential than you think he has.

ADVICE FROM THE QUEENS

If a woman can receive advice from the kings, a man can receive advice from the queens in virtually the same way. The pack is shuffled and the four queens selected. A die is chosen, and after being kissed, is dropped onto the queens. The only difference is that a man interprets the die when an odd number is showing on the top.

Queen of Spades

If the die rests on this card with a one-spot uppermost, you will meet a fair-haired woman who will bring you great happiness.

If the die rests on this card with a three-spot uppermost, you will experience a disappointment with a dark-haired woman.

If the die rests on this card with a five-spot uppermost, you will have difficulty in extricating yourself from an unsuitable relationship.

Queen of Diamonds

If the die rests on this card with a one-spot uppermost, you will receive the affection of someone who does not appeal to you.

If the die rests on this card with a three-spot uppermost, you will become involved with an intriguing, but potentially dangerous, woman.

If the die rests on this card with a five-spot uppermost, you are about to meet someone who will bring you great happiness.

Queen of Hearts

If the die rests on this card with a one-spot uppermost, you need to beware of the maneuverings of an older woman who is working against you.

If the die rests on this card with a three-spot uppermost, a girl you are keen on will turn you down.

If the die rests on this card with a five-spot uppermost, you will become involved with a jealous woman. This relationship will prove difficult, but will not last.

Queen of Clubs

If the die rests on this card with a one-spot uppermost, you must be careful in any dealings with a dark-haired woman who seems too good to be true.

If the die rests on this card with a three-spot uppermost, an older woman will provide help, counsel, and good advice.

If the die rests on this card with a five-spot uppermost, you will meet a young woman who quickly falls in love with you.

WILL THE PERSON OF MY DREAMS ARRIVE IN THE NEXT TWELVE MONTHS?

One of the cards is chosen to represent the man or woman of your dreams. The cards are thoroughly shuffled. Twelve cards are dealt out in a row, and then another twelve cards are dealt on top of these. This is continued until all the cards have been dealt. Each pile represents one of the next twelve months.

Starting with the first month, the piles are turned over to see which month contains the card symbolizing the special person. Once the month has been determined, the other cards in the pile are interpreted to see how the relationship will develop.

Let's assume that you used the king of hearts to represent your future lover. This card was in the seventh pile, indicating that you will meet him in seven months' time. The other cards in this pile are the three of clubs, eight of spades, and ten of hearts. The three of clubs is a sign of temporary unpleasantness, indicating that you may be snubbed or become the victim of malicious gossip. Despite being a spade, the eight of spades is a happy card, indicating joy, contentment, and material success. The ten of hearts is a sign of good news. This indicates that although the initial meeting will not go too well, you will receive some positive news that clarifies the situation. The unpleasantness will be forgotten, and the relationship will prove a happy and enjoyable one.

SIX PATHS TO HAPPINESS

This method assumes that you have already found the right person, and want confirmation that the relationship will continue to grow and develop. This method is popular as it involves both a poem and a kiss. The poem is:

> One pile for me,
> And one for thee.
> One for health,
> And next for wealth.
> One pile for friends,
> (Add a kiss to the blend)
> And a pile for love that never ends.

It is important that the deck of cards is complete, and contains the joker. Choose a card to represent you, and then another to symbolize your partner. Think about your relationship while shuffling the cards, and silently ask any questions that you would like to have answered.

Cut the pack with your left hand, and then hold the deck facedown. Say the first line of the rhyme out loud and deal the top card of the deck facedown onto the table as you say the last word of the line. Recite the second line, and deal the next card to the right of the first card as you say the final word of the line. Repeat with the next three lines, saying the words while dealing the cards in a rhythmical manner. No card is dealt when you say the sixth line ("Add a kiss to the blend"). After saying this line, kiss the top card of the pack—ideally with a flourish—and deal this card when saying the final word of the poem.

You should end up with six cards lined up in a row in front of you. Repeat the rhyme, dealing the cards on top of the cards that have already been dealt. Continue doing this until all the cards have been dealt. As there are fifty-three cards in the deck, and six piles of cards, you will have only five cards left to deal when you repeat the poem for the last time. Consequently, when you say, "Add a kiss to the blend," kiss your fingers, and rest them lightly on the sixth pile as you say the final word.

Turn over the top card of each pile, and interpret them using the meaning of the card and the relevant line of the poem. Naturally, for the purposes of love and romance, piles one, two, and six are the most important ones. If the top cards of each pile do not provide enough information, turn over as many cards as necessary to provide the detail you need.

Finally, look at all the cards in piles one, two, and six to see if the cards that represent you and your lover are included in these piles. If you find them both in these three piles, your future together is assured. If one of them is found here, the future looks good, but the relationship needs more work. If neither card is found in these three piles, you need to think carefully about the long-term future of your relationship.

I have found this method astonishingly accurate. Many years ago, I did this for an engaged couple. They appeared to be extremely happy, but neither of their cards appeared in piles one, two, or six. This was embarrassing for me at the time, but I knew enough to implicitly trust the cards. The cards were uncannily prophetic. The couple got married, but separated just a few months later.

On another occasion, I did this for a couple who were experiencing problems in their relationship. Both of their cards were in the sixth pile, indicating a "love that never ends." Every now and again I see this couple in a shopping mall near my home. They are always arm-in-arm and appear extremely happy.

In the next chapter we will look at some spreads that can be used for other purposes.

eight

OTHER SPREADS

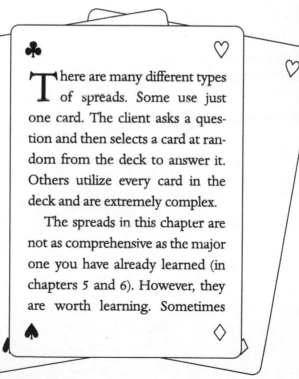

There are many different types of spreads. Some use just one card. The client asks a question and then selects a card at random from the deck to answer it. Others utilize every card in the deck and are extremely complex.

The spreads in this chapter are not as comprehensive as the major one you have already learned (in chapters 5 and 6). However, they are worth learning. Sometimes you may not have time to do a complete reading. You may feel that a certain spread will be better at answering a specific question than another. You may simply like one spread more than the others. Practice them all and see which spreads appeal most to you.

Past-Present-Future

Mix the cards while thinking of your question. Cut the pack three times. Deal fifteen cards into three piles of five cards each, and place the rest of the deck to one side (Figure 6). The cards in the left-hand pile represent the past, the cards in the center pile reveal the present, and the cards in the right-hand pile indicate the future.

Turn over the cards that represent the past. Start by interpreting each card individually, and then see if you can arrange them to create a story that relates to your past. It is easier to do this if you use a keyword for each card. You may, for example, have the nine of diamonds, three of hearts, king of hearts, ace of clubs, and the six of diamonds. If we turn these cards into keywords we get: wishes come true (9D); disappointments in love (3H); a wise man (KH); ambitions, hopes, and dreams (AC); and a happy home life (6D). These cards can be connected in different ways, but it appears that this person came from a good home (6D), with a good and wise father (KH). Although there have been disappoint-

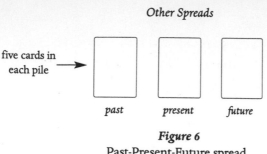

five cards in
each pile → past   present   future

Figure 6
Past-Present-Future spread.

ments in love (3H), this person remains positive and ambitious (AC), and believes that his or her dreams will come true (9D).

The cards for the present are then turned over and interpreted in the same way. Finally, the cards indicating the future are turned over and interpreted.

If the cards do not provide sufficient information, fifteen more cards can be dealt out into three piles. These cards reveal your subconscious motivations, and can be extremely revealing. A large number of spades, for instance, reveals inner turmoil, even though outwardly the person may appear calm and serene.

DATE OF BIRTH READING

This method is called the Date of Birth reading as it uses your date of birth to locate three cards, which are then interpreted (Figure 7). Mix the cards slowly while thinking of a question you want answered. When you feel the cards have been mixed enough, deal a pile of

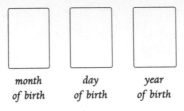

month	day	year
of birth	*of birth*	*of birth*

Figure 7
Date of Birth spread.

cards facedown that relates to your month of birth. If you were born in January, deal just one card, as January is the first month of the year. You would deal three cards for March, nine for September, and so on.

To the right of this pile deal another pile that relates to your day of birth. If you were born on the third of the month, you would deal three cards. If your day of birth was the twenty-eighth, you would deal twenty-eight cards.

Finally, deal another pile that relates to your year of birth. First, you have to turn your year of birth into a single digit. I was born in 1946. Consequently, I would add 1 + 9 + 4 + 6. This totals 20. I would then add 2 + 0 to arrive at a single digit. I would deal two cards in the final pile.

Let's take another example. Assume you were born in 1979. 1 + 9 + 7 + 9 = 26, and 2 + 6 = 8. You would deal eight cards in the final row. If you were born in 1984, you would deal four cards in the final row, and if you were born in 1963, you would deal just one card in the final row.

You now turn over the top card of each pile and interpret it. All three cards relate to the next few months. It is not correct to assume the card on the left-hand pile indicates the first month, the middle pile the second, and the right-hand pile the third. All three cards relate to all three months.

It is interesting to note that every date of birth can be covered by the fifty-two cards in the deck. Someone born on December 31, 1989, would have twelve cards in the first pile, thirty-one in the second, and nine in the third. This totals fifty-two and is the highest number possible to reach with this reading method.

BIRTHDAY READING

This reading can be done only once a year, on your birthday. The method is exactly the same as the Date of Birth reading, except that instead of using your year of birth for the third pile, you use the current year (Figure 8). For 2003, you would deal five cards in the final pile.

The three cards will give you the general trends for the following twelve months. Consequently, you can immediately follow up by doing the Date of Birth reading to get more specific information about the next three months.

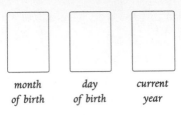

month | day | current
of birth | of birth | year

Figure 8
Birthday spread.

GYPSY SPREAD

I learned this particular spread while living in Cornwall, England, in the late 1960s, and have found it useful for doing quick readings. It can be used for giving a quick look at the past, present, and future. Alternatively, it can be used to answer specific questions.

The deck is thoroughly shuffled and placed on the table. About half of the deck is cut off and placed on the table above the remaining cards. This creates two piles of cards. The cards that are furthest away from you are then cut in half again, and these cards are placed to the left of the two piles on the table. The cards in the pile nearest you are also cut in half, and these cards are placed to the right, creating four piles of cards, each containing approximately one quarter of the deck (Figure 9). The pile to your left represents the past. There are two piles in the center. The one closer to you represents the present situation. The other pile

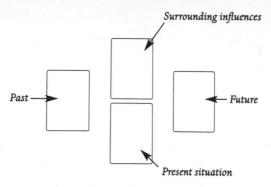

Surrounding influences

Past →

← *Future*

Present situation

Figure 9
Gypsy spread.

represents influences that are currently surrounding you. The pile to the right represents the future.

The ritual is not complete yet. Pick up the pile to the left (the past), and deal the top three cards facedown in the position the past pile had been in. Deal the next card on top of the pile clockwise to the right (surrounding influences), followed by the other two piles (future and present situation). Then replace the remaining cards in your hand on top of the three cards you dealt initially. The same thing happens with the pile that represents the influences that are currently surrounding you: three cards are dealt in a pile, and the next three cards are dealt on top of the other three piles. This is repeated twice more, first with the pile representing the future, followed by the pile representing the present.

Finally, the top card of each pile is turned over and interpreted. For a quick reading, these four cards are all that are required. However, if necessary, the next two cards in each pile can be interpreted as well.

I am frequently asked why three cards are placed on the bottom of the pile, and the next three cards dealt to the other piles. I asked the same question myself on several occasions, and never received a satisfactory answer. I was told that it was "tradition," or that it had always been done that way. The answer is probably related to the fact that throughout the world the number three has always been connected with divinity. The Christian trinity of Father, Son, and Spirit is an obvious example. Other examples are the Hindu trinity of Brahma, Vishnu, and Siva (Creator, Preserver, and Changer), and Osiris, Isis, and Horus in the Egyptian tradition. In the Wiccan tradition, the three great mysteries are birth, life, and death. Christians have the three virtues of faith, love, and hope. In folklore, the expression "third-time lucky" is very old, showing the powerful symbolic effect this number continues to have on all of us. Yet another possibility is that in olden times the living were referred to as "three times blessed." (The dead were known as "four times blessed.")

THE MYSTIC CROSS

There are many versions of the Mystic Cross, each using a different number of cards. This method of fortune telling is extremely popular in Europe, which is where I first saw it. The version I saw uses thirteen cards.

Start by shuffling the cards thoroughly, and then deal seven cards facedown in a horizontal row in front of you. The middle card of this row will also become the middle card of the vertical row that consists of three cards dealt above this central card and three below. (In some versions of this spread, the center card is the client's significator card.)

This gives us a Mystic Cross comprising thirteen face-down cards. Turn over the center card first, and then turn over all the cards in the vertical row, followed by the cards in the horizontal row.

The cards in the vertical row represent the present situation and the influences that are surrounding the querent. They are read first, from top to bottom. The cards in the horizontal row modify the reading of the cards in the vertical row. In some ways, they also give a sense of time to the reading. The cards to the left of the central card relate generally to the past, while the cards to the right indicate unexpected happenings in the future.

Recently, I used this spread to help an elderly woman who wanted to visit a sick sister overseas, but was unsure whether or not to make the trip. The spread we created is shown in Figure 10.

The first thing I noticed was the three nines in the vertical row. This is a sign of happiness and fulfillment, and is usually unexpected. Because this happiness is the

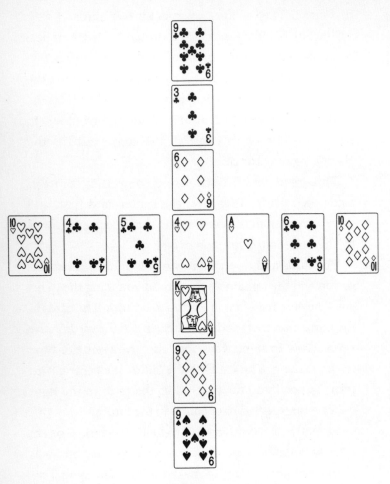

Figure 10
Mystic Cross spread example.

result of a change in attitude, it appears that my client, or someone close to her, will be changing his or her mind about something. The nine of clubs indicates that the client is looking for a new challenge. However, the three of clubs shows that she might experience some temporary unpleasantness. The six of diamonds shows my client enjoyed a happy home life, and was possibly unsure about whether or not to leave it, even to visit a sick sister.

The four of hearts in the center shows that the client will receive satisfaction and pleasure from helping her sister. The king of hearts indicates a strong man in her life. I thought my client was a widow, and asked her about this man.

"That's my brother Tom," she replied. "He's in poor health, so can't travel. He's pushing for me to make the trip."

The nine of diamonds is a positive card as long as the client's desires are worthwhile. This is obviously the case with this reading. The final card in the vertical row was the nine of spades, not usually a positive card. However, it indicates an unexpected change. After looking at those cards, it seemed certain to me that my client would make the trip, but it would probably be a spur-of-the-moment decision. However, once she made her mind up and embarked on the trip, she would receive great joy and satisfaction from visiting and helping her sister.

The horizontal row tended to bear this out. The ten of hearts is a sign of good news. On the left-hand side of this row, this probably related to the past. My client told me that her sister had survived an operation that usually proved fatal. The four and five of clubs were interesting. The four showed my client would receive help from others, but the five indicated a disagreement. It turned out that both of these related to her brother. He wanted her to take the trip, but he also wanted her close to attend to his needs.

The ace of hearts was in the near future and promised happiness and pleasant times with family and friends. This indicated that the trip was not far away. The six of clubs showed that my client would gain new friends, and also become more relaxed and easy-going. The final card was the ten of diamonds. It showed that my client was paying too much attention to the material side of life. She confessed that she desperately wanted to make the trip, but was concerned about how much it would cost.

Partly as a result of this reading, Beverly made the trip. It proved extremely worthwhile and rewarding. She was able to help her sister recuperate from her illness, and in the process they became closer than ever before.

I have no way of knowing if Beverly would have taken the trip without consulting me. However, the reading, which took less than ten minutes, enabled her to look at all sides of the situation before making up her mind.

YES OR NO

People often want to make a wish when they see cards being read. This is a quick and easy way to see if a person's wish will come true.

The person needs to silently make a wish while slowly shuffling the cards. The cards are then held facedown and dealt faceup one at a time. There are only two cards to consider: the nine of hearts (the wish card) and the ten of spades (the disappointment card). If the wish card appears first, the person's wish will come true. Unfortunately, the opposite is the case if the disappointment card appears first.

If the disappointment card appears first, the person can make another wish (as long as it is on a completely different subject), and try again.

THE SANDWICH

Mentally choose a significator card to represent yourself: a jack if you are under the age of twenty-five, and a king or queen if you are older. Think about your question while slowly and methodically mixing the cards. When you feel the cards are sufficiently mixed, spread the cards between your hands until you find your significator card. Look at the cards on either side of your significator card and interpret them. Occasionally, the significator card will be at the top or bottom of the deck.

In this case, the second card to be interpreted will be at the other end of the deck. Alternatively, you can cut the deck, and spread the cards again.

ONE-TWO-THREE-FOUR-FIVE

This method is similar to the Sandwich, but uses up to five cards. Choose a significator card to represent yourself, and then mix the cards thoroughly while thinking about your question. Stop mixing when you feel the time is right. Hold the deck of cards facedown, and deal the cards faceup in pairs. (In other words, turn over two cards at a time.) Stop doing this when your significator card appears. Interpret the card that appears with your significator card. Stop at this point if the card satisfactorily answers your question. If it does not, turn over the next card and add it to your interpretation. You can turn over up to five cards, if necessary.

ONCE A WEEK

This is a useful method to see what the next seven days will be like. Place the client's significator card on the table. Have him or her shuffle the cards while thinking about the week ahead. Take the cards back and deal out seven cards in a circle around the significator card (Figure 11). Carry on dealing until each of the seven piles contains three cards.

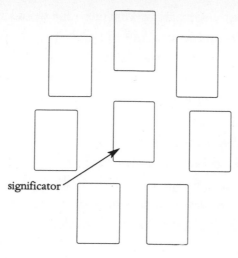

significator

Figure 11
Once a Week spread.

The first pile dealt relates to tomorrow. Pick up the three cards and interpret them. The second pile relates to the day after tomorrow, and so on.

A lady I knew who used this method regularly asked her clients to make a silent wish while shuffling the cards. If the wish card (nine of hearts) appeared in one of the seven piles it was a sign that the wish would be granted.

THE PYRAMID OF EGYPT

The Pyramid of Egypt is used mainly to provide information about the next month. The client shuffles the cards while thinking about what he or she would like to have happen in the next four to five weeks. He or she then cuts the cards, and hands the deck to you.

You then create a pyramid of seven rows of face-down cards (Figure 12). The first row contains one card, the second two, the third three, and so on until seven rows have been dealt to create a pyramid. Once this has been done, gather up the last card dealt in each row, starting with the right-hand card in the bottom row. This gives you seven cards, which are turned over and interpreted. The other cards are discarded.

Experiment with these different spreads. You might want to create some original spreads of your own. This is all part of the joy that comes from reading cards. It is useful to have several different spreads at your disposal. Frequently, I start out with the intention of using a certain spread, but change my mind at the last moment. I have learned that it pays to follow these feelings, and I invariably give a better reading as a result.

Figure 12
The Pyramid of Egypt spread.

AFTERWORD

You now know everything necessary to read cards for both yourself and others. Practice as often as you can. You will find willing volunteers everywhere you go. Like everything else, your skills will develop the more you exercise them.

Remain aware that you are not perfect and will make mistakes. Everyone makes mistakes. If you are prepared to learn from them, they will occur less frequently as you gain experience. Ask the people you read for to give you feedback. Keep a record of the readings you do for yourself. By analyzing these, you will gain valuable information that you can use in future readings.

Remind your clients that they, themselves, are responsible for their own destinies. You cannot make decisions for other people. You can guide them, offer advice, and listen. You can tell them what the cards indicate. However, ultimately, they have to make their own decisions.

Naturally, you will have to be honest, tactful, caring, and sympathetic. You also need to be psychically aware. Use your intuition along with what the cards tell you. You will be amazed at what comes through when you allow your intuition to flow.

Be gentle with your clients. Focus on the positive. Give your readings seriously, but have fun in the process.

Fortune telling has been practiced for thousands of years. By learning how to read playing cards, you are entering a tradition that has stood the test of time, and has helped countless people throughout the ages. I wish you great success with it.

DREAM INTERPRETATION USING PLAYING CARDS

Dreams have fascinated people throughout history. There are numerous examples of how dreams have changed people's lives, and even changed the course of history. The dreams of Joseph, recorded in the book of Genesis, come into this category. However, there are myriad other examples. It is said that Hannibal dreamed of a military victory. King Richard III had prophetic nightmares that predicted his death at Bosworth Field. (Shakespeare made good use of this fact in his play *Richard III*.) Napoleon dreamed of his defeat at the Battle of Waterloo. Abraham Lincoln dreamed of his death a few days before he was murdered. Bishop Joseph Lanyi dreamed of the assassination of his friend, Archduke

Ferdinand, a pivotal event that led to World War I. The bishop recorded his dream and tried to warn the archduke, but was too late.[1]

A great deal of creativity can be attributed directly to dreams. Samuel Taylor Coleridge wrote his famous poem *Kubla Khan* after waking from an opium-induced sleep. He wrote fifty-four lines without effort, but was then interrupted. When he returned to his poem, no more words would come. Robert Louis Stevenson claimed that much of his work was created while in a dream. *The Strange Case of Dr. Jekyll and Mr. Hyde* is his most famous example.

In the book of Job, we are told how God speaks to us in our dreams: "For God speaketh once, yea twice, yet man perceiveth it not. In a dream, in a vision of the night, when deep sleep falleth upon men, in slumberings upon the bed; Then he openeth the ears of men, and sealeth their instruction" (Job 33:14–16).

We all dream, and there are many books available to help us interpret them. However, it can be frustrating to wake up in the morning unable to remember what we were dreaming about. Fortunately, there are three methods that can help us recapture the message or essence of our dreams. They all involve playing cards.

GUIDED BY THE CARDS

This method is similar to a meditation, and is intended to allow the complete memory of the dream to return to you. Think of your desire to remember your dream while casually mixing a deck of cards. When you feel the time is right, deal out five rows of five cards face-down in front of you. Place the other cards to one side, as they will not be used.

Pass your left hand, if you are right-handed, over the five rows of cards and allow your fingers to touch any card. (If you are left-handed, use your right hand.) Turn over this card, and look at it casually. Think about the interpretation of this card, and see if it brings back any memory of your dream.

If, for example, you turned over the two of clubs, you would think about the standard meaning of this card, and how it indicates an invitation that opens the way to further opportunities. You would then pause and see if this thought was recognized by your subconscious mind. If it is, memories of your dream will instantly return to your conscious mind.

However, if this does not occur, you have to pass your hand over the cards again and allow your fingers to select as many cards as are necessary until one creates a response.

Most of the time, you will remember your dream before a dozen cards have been turned over. However, it is possible to go through all twenty-five cards and receive no response from any of them. This is a sign that it is better for you not to recall the dream at this time. This can be disappointing, but shows that your subconscious mind is looking after you twenty-four hours a day. If it was beneficial for you to remember the dream, your subconscious mind would allow it to occur.

MEDITATION METHOD

Meditation is a wonderful way to find out about yourself and the world. There are many ways of meditating, and you probably know of people who meditate while looking at Tarot cards. Ordinary playing cards can be used in exactly the same way. All you need to do is sit down, choose a card at random, and then quietly look at it. Think about the meaning of the card. Look at the placement of the indices and the pips. See what comes into your conscious mind while you are casually examining the card. Doing this on a regular basis will provide you with added insights into the meanings of each card. This will enable you to give more accurate and incisive readings.

We are going to use the meditation method to help recover our lost dreams. Start by quietly sitting down in a place where you will not be disturbed. Casually mix the cards while thinking about your need to remember the dream.

Ask yourself what area of life your dream covered. If it involved love, sex, happy times, and fun activities, the suit of hearts would cover it. If it involved money, position, power, and a forward progression, the suit of diamonds would apply. The clubs relate to creativity and hard work, and the spades relate to change, mystery, confusion, warnings, and unpleasant dreams.

You may not consciously know what area of life your dream covered, but going through the suits in this way will probably create a sense of recognition that gives you a clue. Let's assume that your body responded in some way to the suit of diamonds. Take all the diamond cards out of the deck and arrange them in a straight line in front of you. The cards are dealt in order from ace to king, with the ace on your left and the king on your right.

Look at these cards in a detached, casual way. Study individual cards and see if any of them stimulate your memory. Then, starting with the king, study each card for a few moments and see what it has to tell you. Hopefully, before you reach the last card, your dream will come back to you.

Another way of doing this meditation ritual is to ignore the suits and use the numerological value of the cards. If you feel your dream related to a desire for freedom, place the four fives in front of you and study them. Likewise, if your dream related to communication in any form, study the four threes. I prefer to use the suits rather than the numbers, but I use both methods, depending on what faint memories I have.

GYPSY METHOD

This old Gypsy method was devised to provide meanings for forgotten dreams, as well as to add additional information to dreams that are remembered.

The procedure is a simple one. The cards are thoroughly mixed and cut. The cards are then held facedown, and one card is selected from anywhere in the deck. This card is interpreted, using the meanings in chapter 2.

However, this can also be taken a step further, by using the day of the week and the number of the particular card. (In this system, the jack is 11, the queen 12, and the king 13.)

Each day of the week relates to a particular planet:

Sunday relates to the Sun

Monday relates to the Moon

Tuesday relates to Mars

Wednesday relates to Mercury

Thursday relates to Jupiter

Friday relates to Venus

Saturday relates to Saturn

For instance, you wake up on a Wednesday morning, vaguely remembering that you had a dream of some sort. You mix the cards, cut them, and choose a card at random. This turns out to be the six of hearts. In chapter 2 you read that this card promises a slow, but steady improvement in your circumstances. You will need to be patient, and avoid trying to force things to happen before they are ready.

You now look at the Mercury table in the following pages and see what is listed beside the number six. (This is because Mercury relates to Wednesday and six is the number of the six of hearts.) "You are surrounded by love." This helps clarify the meaning of the six of hearts, as it usually relates to love matters. It appears that you are surrounded by love, whether you are aware of it, or not, and your relationship will slowly, but steadily, improve.

Here is another example. You wake up on a Saturday morning, with only the vaguest memory of your dream. The randomly picked card is the four of clubs. This shows that you will receive help from others whenever it is required. You find it hard to ask others for help, and probably do not realize that others hold you in high regard. You also find it hard to express your emotions. When you look up number four in the Table of Saturn you find, "There is no need to worry. The situation will become clearer in time." This tends to indicate a problem that is concerning you. However, there is no need to worry, as the matter will become clearer in time, and people close to you will be happy to help, if necessary.

As you can see, this system can provide helpful insight into matters that occur in your life, even when you do not remember your dreams. Naturally, the benefits are even greater when you remember the dreams, as you can add these insights to help interpret them.

TABLE OF THE SUN

1. Be prepared for a change. Think before acting.
2. Be patient. Make haste slowly.
3. Someone may be lying.
4. Hard work pays off, but take time off to relax.
5. You are fooling yourself.
6. All close relationships are favored. Be kind.
7. Spend time on your own to think things through.
8. Good fortune is on its way.
9. Think carefully and plan ahead.
10. A new friend is not far away.
11. Don't say everything you know.
12. A chance conversation provides a good opportrnity.
13. Someone you know is a better friend than you realize.

TABLE OF THE MOON

1. The outcome will be favorable.
2. Take time to assess the situation before acting.
3. Don't take matters too seriously.
4. Smooth troubled waters.
5. Exciting opportunity on the horizon.
6. Happiest moments will be at home.
7. Think carefully before acting.
8. Financial advancement possible as long as you act decisively.
9. Temporary setback.
10. The gossip is incorrect. Refuse to listen.
11. Slow, steady progress.
12. A social engagement provides relief from stress.
13. You are on track.

TABLE OF MARS

1. Lady Fortune is smiling on you.
2. Potential for love and romance.
3. Do not hesitate. The time is right.
4. Nothing worthwhile happens without effort.
5. You will be tempted. Think before acting.
6. Someone you have not considered cares about you.
7. Beware of jealousy.
8. Temporary reversal.
9. Happiness is closer than you think.

10. Ultimate success. Two steps forward, one step back.
11. Do what is right.
12. Make a wish. The portents are good.
13. Everything you need is already around you.

TABLE OF MERCURY

1. New financial opportunities are on the horizon.
2. Beware of fair-weather friends.
3. Possibility of travel.
4. Change is necessary, and will provide a better future.
5. Patience is necessary.
6. You are surrounded by love.
7. A chance encounter provides much to think about.
8. Money problems are temporary.
9. An opportunity to learn from experience.
10. Slow progress, but a worthwhile outcome.
11. Avoid rumors and gossip.
12. Seize an opportunity for fun and laughter.
13. Quarrels have no winners.

TABLE OF JUPITER

1. Good fortune.
2. You are worrying unnecessarily.
3. A cheerful friend will offer advice. Listen carefully.
4. Good news from afar.
5. Expect the unexpected.

6. Avoid negative people. Stay positive.
7. Trust your intuition.
8. Money comes after considerable effort.
9. Temporary hiccup passes quickly.
10. Aim high, and keep thinking of your goal.
11. Read the small print. Pay attention to details.
12. Think first, and then make your mind up.
13. Be grateful, and express it to others.

TABLE OF VENUS

1. A change for the better, after a short delay.
2. Possibility of a trip to see old friends.
3. Expect good news.
4. The opportunity you are waiting for is almost here.
5. New insights enable you to look at the situation differently.
6. Love and romance are favored.
7. Take time off to relax and unwind.
8. Young people provide a welcome interlude.
9. Good news for someone close to you.
10. A welcome challenge will present itself.
11. Time for a vacation.
12. A good example is set by someone you hardly know.
13. Time to reassess what is going on in your life.

TABLE OF SATURN

1. Feelings of helplessness will gradually fade.
2. Temporary frustration. Keep calm and in control.
3. Opportunity to make new friends.
4. There is no need to worry. The situation will become clearer in time.
5. Think before acting. Caution is required.
6. Be extravagant.
7. Value the special people in your life.
8. Good news is on its way.
9. The time is right to act. Move forward confidently.
10. Evaluate your ideas carefully. One holds great promise.
11. You are on the right track.
12. Someone is sending kind thoughts your way.
13. An unexpected good turn brings happiness.

NOTES

INTRODUCTION

1. Sir William Wilkinson (1858–1930) had a lengthy career as British consul in China, and became a collector of playing cards. Using the pseudonym of Khanhoo, he wrote several books, including *The Game of Khanhoo* and *Bridge Maxims*. Dr. Stewart Culin (1858–1929) was director of the Museum of Archaeology and Paleontology at the University of Pennsylvania. He wrote *Korean Games, The Gambling Games of the Chinese in America,* and *Chess and Playing Cards.*

2. In his book *A History of Playing Cards,* Roger Tilley speculates that the first European deck may have been created by a miniaturist in northern Italy. This person was probably originally commissioned to create a set of miniature paintings of the local ruling family, and then extended the commission to include other miniatures intended as teaching aids.

3. Kaplan, *The Encyclopedia of Tarot*, 24–25.

4. Tilley, *A History of Playing Cards*, 11.

5. Brother Johannes von Rheinfelden, *Tractatus de moribus et disciplina humanae conversationis*. Unfortunately, the copy of this manuscript in the British Museum is dated 1472. Consequently, the date of 1377 may not be correct.

6. Anonymous, *The Encyclopedia of Occult Sciences*, 220. Although the author insisted on anonymity, the introduction by M. C. Poinsot is written in the same style as the rest of the book. Some accounts of this story credit Agnes Sorel, rather than Odette, with introducing the cards to King Charles VII.

7. Lehmann-Haupt, *Gutenberg*, 89.

8. The hearts, clubs, diamonds, and spades are used in France, the United Kingdom, the United States, and in many other parts of the world. However, in Italy and Spain, cups, swords, coins, and batons are used. In Germany and central Europe, hearts, bells, leaves, and acorns are commonly used. In Switzerland, shields and flowers are used instead of hearts and leaves.

9. Beal, *Playing Cards and Their Story*, 58.

10. Wowk, *Playing Cards of the World*, 142.

11. Grillot de Givry, *Illustrated*, 290–93.

CHAPTER TWO

1. Taylor, *History*, 142. The origins of this story are not known, but Mr. Taylor thought that the first printed version was *Anecdote curieuse et interessante, sous le nom de Louis Bras-de-fer*, which appeared in Brussels in 1778.

2. The first English version of this story was "The Perpetual Almanac or Gentleman Soldier's Prayer Book," printed in the Seven Dials quarter of London about two hundred years ago.

3. For the purposes of simplicity, I refer only to heterosexual partnerships in this book. Naturally, if the client is gay, the cards representing his or her (potential) partner will be of the same sex.

4. There are several other explanations given to explain how this card came to be called the "curse of Scotland." However, the association with the earl of Stair is the most likely one, as his coat of arms included nine lozenge shapes, and he was widely detested because of his association with the Glencoe Massacre.

5. Gattey, *They Saw Tomorrow*, 180.

APPENDIX

1. Fodor, *Encyclopaedia of Psychic Science*, 108–109.

SUGGESTED READING

Anonymous. *The Encyclopedia of Occult Sciences.* New York: Robert M. McBride and Company, 1939.

Beal, George. *Playing Cards and Their Story.* Newton Abbot, U.K.: David and Charles (Holdings) Limited, 1975.

Fodor, Nandor. *Encyclopaedia of Psychic Science.* New Hyde Park, N.J.: University Books, Inc., 1966.

Gattey, Charles Neilson. *They Saw Tomorrow.* London: Granada Publishing Limited, 1977.

Grillot de Givry, Émile. *Illustrated Anthology of Sorcery, Magic and Alchemy.* Translated by J. Courtenay Locke. New York: Causeway Books, 1973. Originally published as *Anthologie de l'Occultisme* (Paris: Editions Chacornac, 1929).

Kaplan, Stuart R. *The Encyclopedia of Tarot.* New York: U.S. Games Systems, Inc., 1978.

Lehmann-Haupt, Hellmut. *Gutenberg and the Master of the Playing Cards.* New Haven, Conn.: Yale University Press, 1966.

Mann, Sylvia. *Collecting Playing Cards.* London: MacGibbon and Kee Limited, 1966.

Taylor, E. S., ed. *The History of Playing Cards with Anecdotes of their use in Conjuring, Fortune-telling and Card-sharping.* London: John Camden Hotten, 1865.

Tilley, Roger. *A History of Playing Cards.* New York: Clarkson N. Potter, Inc., 1973.

Wowk, Kathleen. *Playing Cards of the World: A Collector's Guide.* Guildford, U.K.: Lutterworth Press, 1983.

REACH FOR THE MOON

Llewellyn publishes hundreds of books on your favorite subjects! To get these exciting books, including the ones on the following pages, check your local bookstore or order them directly from Llewellyn.

Order by Phone
- Call toll-free within the U.S. and Canada, 1-877-NEW-WRLD
- In Minnesota, call (651) 291-1970
- We accept VISA, MasterCard, and American Express

Order by Mail
- Send the full price of your order (MN residents add 7% sales tax) in U.S. funds, plus postage & handling to:
  Llewellyn Worldwide
  P.O. Box 64383, Dept. 0-7387-0223-4
  St. Paul, MN 55164–0383, U.S.A.

Postage & Handling
- **Standard** (U.S., Mexico, & Canada)
If your order is:
  $20 or under, add $5
  $20.01–$100, add $6
  Over $100, shipping is free
(Continental U.S. orders ship UPS. AK, HI, PR, & P.O. Boxes ship USPS 1st class. Mex. & Can. ship PMB.)
- **Second Day Air** (Continental U.S. only): $10 for one book plus $1 per each additional book
- **Express** (AK, HI, & PR only) [Not available for P.O. Box delivery. For street address delivery only.]: $15 for one book plus $1 per each additional book
- **International Surface Mail:** $20 or under, add $5 plus $1 per item; $20.01 and over, add $6 plus $1 per item
- **International Airmail:** Books—Add the retail price of each item; Non-book items—Add $5 per item

Please allow 4–6 weeks for delivery on all orders.
Postage and handling rates subject to change.

Discounts
We offer a 20% discount to group leaders or agents. You must order a minimum of 5 copies of the same book to get our special quantity price.

Visit our website at www.llewellyn.com for more information.

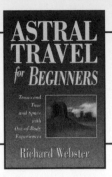

Astral Travel for Beginners
Transcend Time and Space with Out-of-Body Experiences

RICHARD WEBSTER

Astral projection, or the out-of-body travel, is a completely natural experience. You have already astral traveled thousands of times in your sleep, you just don't remember it when you wake up. Now, you can learn how to leave your body at will, be fully conscious of the experience, and remember it when you return.

The exercises in this book are carefully graded to take you step-by-step through an actual out-of-body experience. Once you have accomplished this, it becomes easier and easier to leave your body. That's why the emphasis in this book is on your first astral travel.

The ability to astral travel can change your life. You will have the freedom to go anywhere and do anything. You can explore new worlds, go back and forth through time, make new friends, and even find a lover on the astral planes. Most importantly, you will find that you no longer fear death as you discover that you are indeed a spiritual being independent of your physical body.

By the time you have finished the exercises in this book you will be able to leave your body and explore the astral realms with confidence and total safety.

1-56718-796-X

256 pp., 5³⁄₁₆ x 8 $9.95

To order, call 1-877-NEW WRLD
Prices subject to change without notice

Palm Reading for Beginners
*Find Your Future
in the Palm of Your Hand*

RICHARD WEBSTER

Announce in any gathering that you read palms and you will be flocked by people thrilled to show you their hands. When you are have finished *Palm Reading for Beginners,* you will be able to look at anyone's palm (including your own) and confidently and effectively tell them about their personality, love life, hidden talents, career options, prosperity, and health.

Palmistry is possibly the oldest of the occult sciences, with basic principles that have not changed in 2,600 years. This step-by-step guide clearly explains the basics, as well as advanced research conducted in the past few years on such subjects as dermatoglyphics.

1-56718-791-9
264 pp., 5³⁄₁₆ x 8, illus.   **$9.95**

Soon available in Spanish

Dowsing for Beginners

How to Find Water,
Wealth & Lost Objects

RICHARD WEBSTER

This book provides everything you need to know to become a successful dowser. Dowsing is the process of using a dowsing rod or pendulum to divine for anything you wish to locate: water, oil, gold, ancient ruins, lost objects, or even missing people. Dowsing can also be used to determine if something is safe to eat or drink, or to diagnose and treat allergies and diseases.

Learn about the tools you'll use: angle and divining rods, pendulums, wands—even your own hands and body can be used as dowsing tools! Explore basic and advanced dowsing techniques, beginning with methods for dowsing the terrain for water. Find how to dowse anywhere in the world without leaving your living room, with the technique of map dowsing. Discover the secrets of dowsing to determine optimum planting locations; to monitor your pets' health and well-being; to detect harmful radiation in your environment; to diagnose disease; to determine psychic potential; to locate archeological remains; to gain insight into yourself, and more! *Dowsing for Beginners* is a complete "how-to-do-it" guide to learning an invaluable skill.

1-56718-802-8

256 pp., 5¼ x 8, illus., photos $9.95

Aura Reading for Beginners
Develop Your Psychic Awareness for Health & Success

RICHARD WEBSTER

When you lose your temper, don't be surprised if a dirty red haze suddenly appears around you. If you do something magnanimous, your aura will expand. Now you can learn to see the energy that emanates off yourself and other people through the proven methods taught by Richard Webster in his psychic training classes.

Learn to feel the aura, see the colors in it, and interpret what those colors mean. Explore the chakra system, and how to restore balance to chakras that are over- or understimulated. Then you can begin to imprint your desires into your aura to attract what you want in your life.

1-56718-798-6
208 pp., 5³⁄₁₆ x 8, illus. $9.95

Write Your Own Magic

The Hidden Power in Your Words

RICHARD WEBSTER

This book will show you how to use the incredible power of words to create the life that you have always dreamed about. We all have desires, hopes and wishes. Sadly, many people think theirs are unrealistic or unattainable. *Write Your Own Magic* shows you how to harness these thoughts by putting them to paper.

Once a dream is captured in writing it becomes a goal, and your subconscious mind will find ways to make it happen. From getting a date for Saturday night to discovering your purpose in life, you can achieve your goals, both small and large. You will also learn how to speed up the entire process by making a ceremony out of telling the universe what it is you want. With the simple instructions in this book, you can send your energies out into the world and magnetize all that is happiness, success, and fulfillment to you.

0-7387-0001-0
312 pp., 5³⁄₁₆ x 8 $9.95

Spanish edition:
Escriba su propia magia
0-7387-0197-1 $12.95

To order, call 1-877-NEW WRLD
Prices subject to change without notice

Soul Mates

Understanding Relationships Across Time

RICHARD WEBSTER

The eternal question: how do you find your soul mate—that special, magical person with whom you have spent many previous incarnations? Popular metaphysical author Richard Webster explores every aspect of the soul mate phenomenon in his newest release.

The incredible soul mate connection allows you and your partner to progress even further with your souls' growth and development with each incarnation. *Soul Mates* begins by explaining reincarnation, karma, and the soul, and prepares you to attract your soul mate to you. After reading examples of soul mates from the author's own practice, and famous soul mates from history, you will learn how to recall your past lives. In addition, you will gain valuable tips on how to strengthen your relationship so it grows stronger and better as time goes by.

1-56718-789-7
216 pp., 6 x 9 $12.95

Spanish edition:
Almas gemelas
0-7387-0063-0 $12.95

Is Your Pet Psychic?
Developing Psychic Communication
with Your Pet

RICHARD WEBSTER

Cats who predict earthquakes, dogs who improve marriages, and horses who can add and subtract—animals have long been known to possess amazing talents. Now you can experience for yourself the innate psychic abilities of your pet with *Is Your Pet Psychic?*.

Learn to exchange ideas with your pet that will enhance your relationship in many ways. Transmit and receive thoughts when you're at a distance, help lost pets find their way home, even communicate with pets who are deceased.

Whether your animal walks, flies, or swims, it is possible to establish a psychic bond and a more meaningful relationship. This book is full of instructions, as well as true case studies from past and present.

0-7387-0193-9
288 pp., 5¾₆ x 8 $12.95

Soon available in Spanish:
Los poderes psíquicos de las mascotas
0-7387-0305-2 $12.95

Seven Secrets to Success
A Story of Hope

RICHARD WEBSTER

Originally written as a letter from the author to his suicidal friend, this inspiring little book has been photocopied, passed along from person to person, and even appeared on the Internet without the author's permission. Now available in book form, this underground classic offers hope to the weary and motivation for us all to let go of the past and follow our dreams.

It is the story of Kevin, who at the age of twenty-eight is on the verge of suicide after the failure of his business and his marriage. Then he meets Todd Melvin, an elderly gentleman with a mysterious past. As their friendship unfolds, Todd teaches Kevin seven secrets—secrets that can give you the power to turn your life around, begin anew, and reap success beyond your wildest dreams.

1-56718-797-8

144 pp., 5¾₆ x 8 $6.95

Feng Shui for Beginners

Successful Living by Design

RICHARD WEBSTER

Not advancing fast enough in your career? Maybe your desk is located in a "negative position." Wish you had a more peaceful family life? Hang a mirror in your dining room and watch what happens. Is money flowing out of your life rather than into it? You may want to look to the construction of your staircase!

For thousands of years, the ancient art of feng shui has helped people harness universal forces and lead lives rich in good health, wealth, and happiness. The basic techniques in *Feng Shui for Beginners* are very simple, and you can put them into place immediately in your home and work environments. Gain peace of mind, a quiet confidence, and turn adversity to your advantage with feng shui remedies.

1-56718-803-6
240 pp., 5¼ x 8, photos, diagrams $12.95

To order, call 1-877-NEW WRLD
Prices subject to change without notice